A Maritime History of
SOUTHAMPTON
in picture postcards

Alan Leonard and Rodney Baker

Ensign
PUBLICATIONS

First published in 1989
by Ensign Publications
A division of Hampshire Books Ltd
2 Redcar Street
Southampton SO1 5LL

Printed in the E.E.C.

British Library Cataloguing in Publication Data
Leonard, Alan
    A maritime history of Southampton in picture postcards.
    1. Hampshire. Southampton. Ports: Port of Southampton, history
    I. Title II. Baker, Rodney
    387.1'09422'76

ISBN 1-85455-032-2

Jacket illustrations (front and back).
Southern Railway Posters by Leslie Carr. 1936. (National Railway Museum, York.)

CONTENTS

Introduction	4
Index of Postcard Publishers	6
Gateway to the World	7
Floating Bridge	11
Royal Pier	12
Docks and Railway Companies	17
Growth of the Docks	18
Paddle Steamers	21
Hythe Ferry	23
Town Quay: Redbridge Quay	24
South Western Hotel; the 'time ball'	25
LSWR Steamers	26
Royal Mail Steam Packet Company	27
German Lines	30
Union-Castle Line	31
Shipping Company Sidelights	33
American Line	34
White Star Line	36
Emigrants from Southampton	38
Union-Castle Liners	39
German Liners	40
Shipping Disasters	41
Royal Mail Steamships	49
Arundel Castle	50
Cunard Line Publicity Cards	51
Admiral Sir John Jellicoe: HMS Hampshire	52
Thornycroft Destroyers	53
Troopships	54
Hospital Ships	55
Captain Charles Fryatt, the 'Pirate Dodger'	56
HMS Southampton	57
HMT Czar	58
World War I Train Ferry	59
Aerial Views — Town Quay and Docks	60
Royal Mail Publicity Cards	61
White Star and Cunard-White Star Cards	62
Floating Dry Dock	63
Southern Railway — Public Relations	64
Majestic	65
Aquitania	66
Berengaria	68
Leviathan	69
New Docks: King George V Graving Dock	70
Canadian Pacific Empress Liners	71
Warwick Castle: Arandora Star	73
SR Steamer Dinard: Gracie Fields	74
Bremen and Europa	75
Queen Mary	76
Normandie	78
Dutch Liners	79
Athlone Castle: America	80
Queen Elizabeth	81
Ocean Terminal	83
Cunard Liners Mauretania (II); Caronia	84
New Australia: Andes	85
Shaw Savill Liners	86
Winchester Castle	87
P&O Liners	88
Liberté: Ile de France	89
Dutch Liners	90
Balmoral (II): Coast Lines	91
Ubena/HMT Empire Ken	92
United States	93
From the Amazon	94
The Changing Port Scene	95
Index of Ships	96

INTRODUCTION

The postcards chosen for this book, to illustrate aspects of Southampton maritime history, are a personal selection from many hundreds available but they represent only a fraction of the thousands of cards devoted to port and shipping subjects — and a truly minute proportion of the millions of different cards featuring every possible theme and topic, issued over the past ninety and more years by a host of publishers, local, national and international.

Plain postcards were first issued in Britain in 1870, a year after this form of cheap communication had been pioneered in the old Austro-Hungarian empire. They were 'official' Post Office productions, imprinted with a halfpenny stamp, sold at 6½d. a dozen and also supplied in bulk to commercial users for printing with business messages and advertising. Not until 1894 did the Post Office accept privately produced cards, on which the sender could affix an ordinary adhesive stamp.

This relaxation opened the way for enterprising firms to produce the first British picture postcards — for which a receptive market had been created by the souvenir pictorial cards available over the previous decade at many European hotels, holiday resorts and beauty spots. These colourful and artistic greetings cards, sent home by those able to enjoy holidays abroad, helped to dispel earlier prejudice among the middle and upper classes against postcards, which were initially considered 'vulgar', as well as leaving their correspondence open to the prying eyes of servants and postmen.

The development of picture postcard publishing was for some years hindered by limitations on size and the fact that the picture side had also to allow space for correspondence, since only the address could be written on the back. In 1899 the Post Office raised the permitted size to 5½ by 3½ inches (14 × 9 cm), the standard format already established on the Continent. Further relaxation in P.O. regulations, taken up from 1902, allowed publishers to issue such cards with the picture occupying the whole of one side, half of the address side being ruled off for correspondence. Within a few years, foreign countries also accepted postcards in this style, which greatly increased their utility and popularity.

The extension of literacy following the introduction of compulsory education in the 1870s provided a growing mass market for postcards as a cheap and convenient means of simple correspondence, speedily conveyed by a labour-intensive postal service which afforded five deliveries a day in most urban areas, including Southampton. In pre-telephone days, a young man could safely send a card at lunch time to arrange an evening meeting with his girl; most prosaically, a housewife could post her order to the butcher in the morning, secure in the knowledge that his boy would bring the meat to her door in the afternoon.

Rising living standards, greater mobility and the possibility of real holidays for ordinary folk enlarged the market for picture postcards, which were increasingly exchanged between friends and collectors: in many homes an album became a focus of interest, even a status symbol.

The variety of subjects was immense. Vying with each other, publishers constantly sought to offer something different in style and topic — humorous, sentimental, artistic, patriotic, military, shipping and transport, scenic, topographical, greetings, commemorative and many other themes abounded. Railway and shipping companies, hotels and theatres were among many issuing postcards for publicity purposes.

Some popular magazines included free cards for their readers but in Edwardian times newspapers and periodicals published few photographic illustrations. To fill this gap, many enterprising photographers seized opportunities to rush out topical postcards of local scenes and events, especially dramatic happenings like crashes, fires, floods and shipping disasters, as well as producing cards to order for groups as diverse as laundry workers, football teams and charabanc outings.

These were real photographs, printed in small numbers in sepia or black and white, with or without captions and imprints. Bigger publishers issued long runs of colour cards, which until 1914 were often printed in Germany, sometimes in France or Belgium, where specialist firms offered better and cheaper lithography.

The flood of picture postcards was affected by World War I and abated after 1918, when postage on them went up to a penny — and, briefly, to 1½d. in 1921-22. Postcards, of course, continued to be produced, although in lesser numbers and variety than during their pre-war "Golden Age."

The doyen of Southampton postcard publishers during this period was the splendidly named Franchis Godolphin Osborne Stuart, a Scot from Braemar who pursued his career as a photographer in Aberdeen and London before coming to Southampton around 1883. He first took premises in Bedford Place, moving by 1887 to 57-61 Cromwell Road, where he remained for the rest of his life. His two-storey red brick workshop and studio at No. 61 has stood for over a century but may soon be demolished for new house building.

Stuart began publishing postcards in 1901, drawing on his large stock of photographs previously contributed to local annuals and guidebooks and the London magazine *Army & Navy Illustrated*. Its publisheres, Hudson & Kearns, printed his early cards in black and white, as also some later cards, but from 1903 he had most of them lithographed in Germany by a printer, as yet unidentified, whose delicate and realistic colours enhanced Stuart's photographic artistry.

His main numbered series comprised over 2,000 cards. Most were topographical and scenic, half being of Southampton and Hampshire places, with others extending over several Southern counties and including nearly 300 devoted to shipping subjects. Stuart cards retailed at a penny; competition was fierce and profit margins small, which may explain the poorer quality of German reprints from about 1910. After 1914, Stuart's British-printed cards reflect wartime production difficulties at home.

Stuart's business was carried on through the Twenties and Thirties by his daughter Flora and son-in-law Charles Dowson, who kept a newsagent's shop in Carlton Place. Some good quality "real photograph" cards of Southampton scenes were issued during this period.

Altogether, some 2,500 cards appeared with the imprint of F.G.O. Stuart, now much esteemed by collectors. Foremost among them is Mr. J.H. Foley of Woolston, who has researched and written the authoritative account of Stuart cards (in *Picture Postcard Annual,* 1985) and is compiling a detailed checklist of them.

Another early publisher of postcards depicting Southampton landmarks, docks, shipping and scenes in the surrounding villages was Whitfield Cosser, in business as a photographer at Hanover Buildings during 1902-05 and afterwards at Salisbury and Devizes. From 1903 he issued many fine cards, in enduring sepia on good quality stock. The booming postcard market allowed him to risk undermining his own sales by supplying prints of the same photographs several times over to various 'national' publishers for them to use in their own series — mostly coloured. Bigger firms, mainly London-based, found it uneconomic to send their own photographers all around the country and often bought suitable pictures from local photographers like Cosser, whose work was evidently well regarded.

Cosser's original photograph of the memorial to the *Stella* stewardess Mrs. Rogers on the Western Esplanade (page 41) was used for a baker's dozen of different cards from other publishers, right up to 1917. (For a detailed account, see article in *Picture Postcard Magazine*, November 1987). One hopes Mr. Cosser was well rewarded, even if he did not get royalties on all the many cards reproducing his work!

Mentor & Co., photographers in Oxford Street from about 1890 to 1908, issued some neat cards around 1905. Adolph Rapp began trading in Bernard Street in 1908 as a 'foreign bookseller' but within a few years became a 'marine photographer': until leaving the scene about 1915 he produced a number of cards, mostly to private order, including cricket and football teams as well as shipping subjects. Also in Bernard Street was the studio of George W. Latter, whose family photographic business was the oldest in town, dating back to 1857 and continuing there until 1914. Latter was another marine photographer, who issued postcards of ships.

Miss G.A. Pratt initially worked for John Adams, the booksellers (whose trade also included postcards), in Oxford Street for over a century from the 1850s, more recently in St. Mary Street. In 1910 she set up on her own a few doors away, as a 'nautical bookseller'; she issued shipping cards, with her own distinctive wheel insignia. Max Mills, who produced topical postcards from 1904, was the business name of Wilfrid Ashby, a talented artist and musician as well as photographer. He had his studio in East Park Terrace from 1898, moving after ten years to Rockstone Place, where he continued high class work until 1939.

The variety in style of the many colourful and artistic cards bearing the name of C.J. Bealing show that this local publisher ordered them selectively from various sources; many are quality productions from European printers, while some reproduce Cosser photographs. Clarence John Bealing was evidently a man of parts; beginning as an outfitter's assistant, he went on to run a temperance hotel in Northam through the 1890s, then 'refreshment rooms' at St. Denys in 1903-05; while directories listed him as an insurance agent (living in Portswood and Highfield), he diversified his interests — his advertising card of 1906-08 described him as "wholesale haberdasher, stationer, general sundries-man and pictorial postcard publisher. Speciality — glossy local views; also agent for Stuart coloured local views." Bealing began issuing his own cards about 1906; by 1908 the imprint changed to Bealing & Hickson — presumably James R. Hickson, listed as a newsagent in Shirley until 1912, when the partners seem to have ended their Southampton business.

In the decades before and after World War I, Rood Bros. (originally A.E. Rood & Co.), wholesale stationers in Bevois Valley Road from 1907 until the Sixties, published a wide range of postcards, both photographic and printed, showing scenes in and around Southampton. The old-established firm of G. Buxey/Buxey's Ltd. also published and distributed postcards, while Edwin Jones & Co. sold cards of their own as well as others.

Across the Itchen, several hundred cards of local scenes, buildings, people and occasions — mainly photographic but some machine-printed — were published between about 1905 and 1920 by James Thomas Eltringham of Woolston. Son of a shipwright, who moved his family there from Tyneside about 1875, he was first listed from 1900 as an insurance and estate agent but soon concentrated on photography, with a shop in Portsmouth Road. He retired about 1923, continuing to live in the Bitterne-Sholing area until his death during World War II. Mr. I.P. Presland, secretary of the Southampton Postcard Club, has made a speciality of collecting and researching Eltringham cards.

Some noteworthy contributions to the Southampton postcard output before World War I were made by men who were not primarily photographers. G.D. Courtney, who produced cards showing his keen eye for topical scenes around town and in the docks, kept a chemists's shop in Derby Road for 35 years up to 1939. Herbert Willsteed lived for many years in Brinton's Terrace and worked for Royal Mail, becoming its chief baggage handler. He issued over 300 cards, mostly in 1906-14. Carrying his plate camera around on his bicycle, he photographed many evocative Edwardian scenes in Southampton and neighbourhood. Willsteed had no studio; his cards were produced by a local chemist. Willsteed was still using some of them for personal correspondence up to his death in 1974 — at 90, in an old people's home on the Isle of Wight.

Several more part-time photographers are known to have issued postcards in small numbers, while others produced them without identifying themselves. Most Southampton commercial photographers supplied postcards to order, rather than for general sale, notably Nellie G. Smith, who took over in 1912 the West End Studio in Commercial Road from Chalkley, Gould & Co., who had published a series of cards around 1905. Short & Millard, also in Commercial Road between 1922 and 1938, published a number of cards, while S. A. Chandler & Co., who moved there in 1931, had issued some topical cards soon after opening their Above Bar Studio in 1910.

Many other names on the backs of Southampton postcards are those of retailers, who ordered them in batches from commercial publishers. They include the Bargate Toy Bazaar of Gutteridge & Son; C.W. Moor, a newsagent in London Road for over 30 years up to 1932, and even J. Falcoz, hairdresser in Orchard Place before and during World War I. F.T. Lewis, a tobacconist in St. Mary Street from the 1890s to the 1930s, originated some printed view cards in the Twenties.

"C.R. Hoffmann, No.1, The Docks, Southampton," is the imprint on a series of 'real photograph' postcards (numbered 1,001 to 1,313, with some omissions and duplications), issued mainly during 1924- 39, with some post-war additions; they were followed in the Fifties by a dozen others bearing the name of O.W. Hoffmann, who continued the family business after his father's death in 1952. O.W. Hoffman was, in fact, responsible for its postcard side from the outset, initiating it as an enterprising young man of 20 and directing it through 40 years until selling out in 1964, to begin the active retirement he still enjoys.

Apart from some Southampton scenes photographed one day in 1925 (by A.G. Butler, then in business at Northam), Hoffmann cards concentrated on shipping subjects. Well produced in uniform style by the London printers Wildt & Kray, these glossy sepia cards reproduced photographs (many taken by O.W. Hoffmann himself, some by Beken of Cowes, others supplied by shipping lines) which provide valuable pictorial documentation of many diverse passenger vessels during their 'golden age', usually with detailed captions. Now esteemed by collectors and maritime historians world-wide, Hoffmann cards provide a major element of this book.

The Hoffmann name was well known in Southampton through three generations, beginning with George Heinrich Hoffmann, born in Germany in 1835, who was described as a ship's steward when he married a local girl in 1863. He settled in the town, first as a shopkeeper, later as the proprietor of a hotel in Oriental Place, Canute Road.

His son, Charles Reginald Hoffmann, was an inn-keeper on his own account before setting up as a high-class tobacconist in Oxford Street in 1920. Leaving grammar school that year, young Origen William Hoffmann sought a wider sphere of activity in his father's business, which he soon extended by opening the first shop in the Docks in 1924 — on a prime site, just inside No. 4 Gate — and diversifying there into wider lines of shop trade as well as postcards.

With a keen eye to topical marketing for cards of the ships in port each day (page 60), he vigorously promoted their sale; by the mid-Thirties there were six Hoffmann shops and kiosks covering both Old and New Docks, while six portable stands provided further sales points. Thousands of cards were bought most days by passengers and visitors, at 2d. each or 7 for 1s. At 6d. each, Hoffman also offered souvenir cards of a dozen big liners, in 'giant' ('Book Post') size, 16 × 25 cm.

The 1989 *Picture Postcard Annual* published a full account of Hoffmann cards by the present writers, who have also produced a detailed checklist of Hoffmann cards.

Acknowledgements

Most of the postcards illustrated in this book come from the writers' own collections but some have kindly been made available by friends and fellow collectors, who have also helped with information about them. We gratefully acknowledge the contributions of J.H. Foley, Bert Moody, R.C.W. Payne, I.P. Presland, J.M. Stockley, B.J. Ticehurst and C. Townsend, also Brian Lund, Editor of *Picture Postcard Magazine* (for help with page 47). We are grateful to John Edgar Mann for his helpful reading of our text and to Tom Holder for photography.

This book incorporates details drawn from many sources, including maritime, shipping and local histories (too numerous to list but in a Southampton context we are particularly indebted to Bert Moody and Arthur Taylor); and newspapers, periodicals, directories and other materials in the Local Studies collection of Southampton Central Library and the archives of the City Records Office.

Copyright photographs reproduced by permission are acknowledged in the captions of the postcards involved. Many of the cards illustrated in this book were issued by publishers who are no longer in existence or whom we have been unable to trace; if we have inadvertently infringed any of their rights, we hope they will excuse us.

Rodney Baker & Alan Leonard

INDEX OF POSTCARD PUBLISHERS/PHOTOGRAPHERS/ARTISTS

Baird (Belfast)	45
Bealing, C.J.	9,14
Beken of Cowes	27,50
Boots	30
Brannon, Philip	14
Cosser, Whitfield	18,34,41
Courtney, G.D.	46,48
Crawford, A.	57
Cribb, S.	47
Cumming, Neville	39,49
Dearden & Wade	83,88,92,94
Dixon, J.A.	50
Eltringham, J.T.	53
Feilden, B.A.	91
Fielder, R.F.	64
Frampton, E.J.	21
Gale & Polden	57
Germain (St. Malo)	42
Gothard, Warner	47
Hoffmann, C.R./O.W. 36,37,60,65,67-92 passim	
Hopkins, S.R.	88
Hotels (Atlantic & Cornish)	38
Judges	72
Kirk (Cowes)	29
Levy, Louis (L.L.)	11,15,16,20,22,23, 32,35,36
Lewis, F.T.	63
London View Co.	12
McDowell, W.	62,76
McNally, T.J.	80
Mann, J.	62
Mentor & Co.	23
Nigh, W.J. (Ventnor)	93
Oakley, J.W.	54
Peel, Robert	9
Photochrom Co.	52,60
Pictorial Stationery Co.	44
Picture Postcard Co.	31
Rapp, A.	33
Reid, A. & Co.	26
Revyn, J. (Brussels)	56
Roberts & Wrate	80
Rood Bros.	48
Salmon, J.	88
Shipping Lines	
American	34
Blue Star	73
Coast	91
Cunard	51,66
Cunard-White Star	62,67,76
French	89
Holland-America	79
Red Funnel	74,91
Royal Mail	61
Royal Rotterdam Lloyd	79
Union-Castle	49,87
White Star	62
Shoesmith, Kenneth	61
Short & Millard	25
Smith, W.H.	25
Southern Newspapers	83
Southern Railway	70
"Spitfire"	8
Stengel & Co. (Berlin)	16,39
Stuart, F.G.O.	10,11,13,17,19,27,28,31, 32,36,40,43,44,45,52,55
Turner, Charles	51
Tuck, Raphael	39,49
Valentine & Co.	24,26
Waterlow & Sons	49
Welch, J.	8
Willsteed, H.	24
Woolstone Bros.	12

Note Many of the cards illustrated in this book were issued anonymously, as noted in the captions to them.

The Gateway to the World

Between the wars, in the heyday of great international ocean liners, Southampton was dubbed England's "Gateway to the World." Then handling nearly half the total ocean passenger traffic of the U.K., it owed its leading position to a sequence of dock developments initiated in early Victorian times, taking advantage of an unusually favourable location.

Southampton stands at the head of a deep inlet sheltered by the Isle of Wight, with its deep water harbour benefiting from a remarkable double tide effect which gives extended periods of rising or standing water. These natural advantages facilitated construction of extensive open docks, the basis for the rapid growth of the port in the 19th century, particularly as steamships steadily increased in size and required more navigable deep water.

Much earlier, its sheltered position had attracted sea-borne settlement and trade at three sites within the modern city. The Roman supply base at Clausentum, Bitterne Manor, on the east side of Itchen, and the Saxon town of Hamwic, on the west, in the St. Mary's area, were important in their times but these forerunners had no continuity with the port which later occupied the south-west part of the peninsula between the rivers Itchen and Test. Whatever may have been the link between Hamwic and its successor Hamtun, established there by about 1000 AD, the medieval town that developed after the Norman Conquest represents the decisive third phase in Southampton's maritime history as the urban area around which the modern port grew.

By the 13th century, Southampton had become one of the leading English ports, with a sizeable trade, both coastal and foreign, centred on importing wine and exporting wool. This trade extended beyond France to Spain and Flanders, while in the 15th century Southampton prospered further as the main port of call for ships from the Italian cities, trading in spices, silks and luxury goods from the East.

Southampton recovered from being attacked and plundered by French raiders in 1338. This raid led to the building of defensive walls and towers along its previously open sea-facing sides; much of these fortifications survive, along with the remains of the fine stone houses, with their large storage vaults, once belonging to the town's rich merchant class.

During the Middle Ages, ships were repaired and built at Southampton, notably six for the King's navy in 1414-20 by William Soper at a dock near the West Quay. The largest vessel of its period was the ill-fated *Grace Dieu*, of 1,400 tons, which was struck by lightning and burnt out on the Hamble in 1439.

For a time Southampton was third only to London and Bristol among English ports but its trade declined greatly during the 16th century, reflecting changes in the patterns of international commerce and the increasing importance of London. In 1588 Southampton pleaded poverty to explain why it could provide only one ship instead of the three wanted by the Crown for the fleet to oppose the Spanish Armada.

In the 17th and 18th centuries the port sustained itself serving only domestic needs, although in times of war a few wooden warships were built, particularly in the 1690s by John Winter, who briefly extended his activities from the West Quay to Chapel and Northam. Southampton had little part in the opening up of the New World across the Atlantic and around 1750 it ranked about twelfth among English ports, with a mainly coastal trade, linked with the Channel Islands and France: the wine trade was still sufficient to enable enterprising men like Richard Taunton and George Robinson to make their fortunes.

After 1750 the port benefited from serving the revival and growth of Southampton in its new-found role as a spa, sea-bathing and residential resort town, fringed by fashionable villas and country houses.

The wars with France (1793-1815) dislocated trade and the packet services by then established with Le Havre, the Channel Islands and the Isle of Wight but the needs of the armies gathered around Southampton promoted its 'service economy'. Admiralty requirements for wooden warships brought contracts to shipyards along the Itchen, also at Redbridge, Bucklers Hard, Bursledon and Hamble — although these activities were specialised and short-lived.

The creation of a board of Harbour Commissioners in 1803 signalled a new phase in port development, in line with the rapid growth of the town, whose population in the early 19th century grew faster than many northern industrial centres.

Southampton's further growth was based on commerce rather than industry — of which it had little beyond coach-building — and especially on the development of communications through the application of steam propulsion, for both railways and ships, linking the port more speedily and conveniently with London and overseas.

Ancient Wool House, Southampton, 14ᵗ Century.

The Westgate, Southampton.

Depicted on this 1904 card issued by J. Welch & Sons of Portsmouth is Southampton's only surviving example of a medieval warehouse. This fine stone building was erected in the late 14th century for the Cistercian monks of Beaulieu Abbey, who were great sheep farmers, to store wool awaiting shipment abroad. In 1407 the Wool House was held by a prominent Southampton merchant, Thomas Middleton, who largely financed the building of the Town Quay, south of the Water Gate at the foot of the High Street.

After Southampton's wool trade declined in Tudor times, the Wool House served as a store for other goods, becoming known as the Alum Cellar. On various occasions in the 18th century it housed French and Spanish prisoners of war — some of whom carved their names on its beams.

Thereafter, the Wool House was used for diverse commercial and industrial purposes, including a short period around 1910 when Eric Rowland Moon worked there on his early — but not very successful — aircraft, the "Moonbeam". Since 1966 the Wool House has — very appropriately — accommodated the city's Maritime Museum.

On this card of the West Gate, small boats can be seen through the archway, on the open water that lapped the Western Esplanade until the scene was altered by major land reclamation, particularly in connection with the construction of the New Docks from the late 1920s.

Through two centuries up to its renovation in 1935, the gate tower was leased as a dwelling, given a homely roof-line that belied its earlier military and maritime importance. Built in the aftermath of the devastating French raid of 1338, it led directly to the West Quay, the main centre of medieval shipping activity. The quay was small and much of the loading .and unloading of cargoes was probably done with lighters owing to the lack of deep water frontage.

Through the West Gate passed some of the forces for the great expedition assembled by Henry V in 1415 to sail to France, en route for the battle of Agincourt. It was probably from the West Quay that the "Pilgrim Fathers" set sail in 1620 to seek a new life across the Atlantic.

This card (one of the "Spithead" series from an un-named publisher) was sent from Southampton to a lady in Cambridge, Mass. on September 10th, 1913, by her friend, evidently off a transatlantic liner, with the news-packed message "All well. Good Weather. A stroll on shore here. Seat at captain's left. Pleasant gentlemen at table."

Southampton's coat of arms symbolises its long maritime history. The earliest official record now surviving is a grant of 1575 but the "ancient arms" then confirmed probably dated from the fourteenth century, when Southampton was an important centre of medieval trade and the port of embarkation for military expeditions to France during the Hundred Years War.

The shield bearing red and white roses (probably adopted in compliment to the Dukes of Lancaster and York) is supported by two golden lions standing in the bows of Tudor ships afloat on the surrounding sea. From the late twelfth century, the town seal featured a merchant ship, such as traded in wool and wine with France, Flanders and Spain — another enduring illustration of Southampton's maritime heritage.

Finely printed and embossed, the card is one of an extensive series of heraldic designs published by Robert Peel of Oxford, about 1904. It carries the retailer's name of J. Burbidge, who for a few years ran the Church Book Depot at 68 Above Bar, until it was taken over in 1906 by H.M. Gilbert & Son, the well-known bookselling family now in its fourth generation of trading in Southampton and Winchester.

Edwardian pride in the rapid expansion of Southampton docks was expressed in the contrasting vignettes of this card, one of a series with a "then and now" theme "printed in the County of Saxony" for distribution by C.J. Bealing.

The top picture, captioned "Southampton Docks, 1850", gives an impression of the original Outer Dock, brought into use in 1842-43, with entrances to the three dry docks constructed in 1846-54 and the Inner Dock, opened in 1851 and enlarged in 1859. The docks of the 1850s appear fussily crowded with the small steamers of that period.

Less animated but more extensive and organised is the complementary scene around the Outer Dock, from a photograph taken about 1905 and used separately for cards issued by Bealing and other publishers. As vessels increased in size and more shipping companies were attracted to Southampton, the Docks Company strove to keep pace with demand by building new quays and docks, notably the Empress Dock, opened in 1890.

This so strained the company's resources that it had to be taken over by the LSWR, which soon undertook further extensions, including the huge dry docks named Prince of Wales (1895) and Trafalgar (1905).

From 1894 — when the Post Office first accepted picture postcards — until 1899, when it authorised the standard 5½ x 3½" size, most early British cards were produced in a squarer format, an inch shorter. Correspondence not then being permitted on the address side, the front had to allow space for it, flanking the pictures — generally a group of small vignettes, as on this early example, colourfully lithographed in Germany for a publisher identified only as "E.J. & Co."

Besides the curious inclusion of Netley Abbey, it featured the docks (from a photograph taken some years earlier by F.G.O. Stuart — see next card) and delicate miniatures of the *New York* and *Solent Queen*.

The 10,500 ton *New York* was built in 1888 for the Inman Line; originally styled *City of New York,* her name was shortened when she was transferred to the American Line in 1893, switching her British terminal from Liverpool to Southampton. Apart from wartime diversions, she made transatlantic runs from Southampton until 1920, when she was sold to a Polish company, which scrapped her in 1923.

She was the first steamer to exceed 10,000 tons, leaving aside Brunel's massive "white elephant" *Great Eastern* of 1860, whose 18,915 tons was not topped until 1901, by the *Celtic*.

Contrasting with the *New York* is the 324 ton paddler *Solent Queen,* which ran Red Funnel coastal excursions and Isle of Wight services from 1889 to 1948 (see page 21).

F.G.O. Stuart began issuing postcards in 1901, drawing on his large stock of photographs built up over the preceding 10-15 years. This one, published about 1904, must date from August or September 1889, for it shows the P & O steamer *Arcadia* in the crowded Outer Dock — before the opening of the Empress Dock provided much-needed additional quays.

Impatient of slow progress in docks extensions during the 1870s, the P & O Company had transferred its operations to the Thames, finally ceasing to call at Southampton in 1881. When the great strike of 1889 for the 'dockers' tanner' (sixpence an hour) closed the port of London for several weeks, the *Arcadia* was among the P & O ships temporarily diverted to Southampton. Local dockers handled such 'blackleg' vessels but a year later staged their own — less successful — strike for higher wages.

The *Arcadia* was one of the four 'Jubilee ships' ordered for the P & O fleet in 1887, combining celebration of the jubilees of both Queen Victoria and the company itself. She and her sisters (named *Victoria, Britannia* and *Oceana*) were all over 6,500 tons, some 1,500 tons more than any of their predecessors.

Picturesquely depicted on a Stuart card of about 1905 is the ancient Crosshouse, now 'listed' and refurbished — a reminder of the old-time ferry across the Itchen, rowed by oarsmen of Itchen Ferry village. They were part of a distinctively separate little community of sailors and fishermen, finally dispersed by German bombs in 1940. The ferrymen formerly paid annual homage to Southampton corporation at the Crosshouse, where "in return for the permission of landing on the demesne of the town, they engaged to carry over gratis the burgesses and their families."

This little round "weatherhouse", with its four inner walls arranged to give some shelter from whatever angle the wind blew, was probably of medieval origin. Tradition ascribed its erection to the bequest of an old lady who caught her death of cold waiting for the ferry boat, at what was then a bleak and exposed spot.

Court Leet records show the townsfolk were much concerned about its repair in Elizabethan times. It was rebuilt in 1634 during the mayoralty of Peter Clungeon, whose initials, the date and the town arms were carved on one of its stones.

The other "Cross House" in Stuart's photograph was the warehouse of timber merchants Tagart, Morgan & Coles — whose vehicles often had problems getting around the old stone building, with only 7 ft. of roadway at its sides.

In 1850 Philip Brannon described the Crosshouse as "an interesting relic of the arrangements and customs superseded by the introduction of steam." The motive force that revolutionised sea and land communications during the preceding quarter century and provided the basis for Southampton becoming a major port, was first applied to paddle steamers. Services from Southampton to Cowes began in 1820, followed by others to the Channel Islands and Le Havre, but many people had their first experience of steam propulsion crossing the Itchen for a penny on the "floating bridge" introduced in 1836.

The company formed in 1833 initially proposed a 17-arch fixed bridge with a central swing section to allow ships to pass. The Admiralty considered navigation would still be impeded and favoured a steam-driven cogwheel and chain ferry of the type already operating across the Dart and Tamar. Revising its plans accordingly, the company arranged with its inventor, the distinguished Devonshire engineer James Meadows Rendel, for delivery of a new 'bridge', costing £5,945. This began service on November 23rd, 1836, ceremonially opened in the presence of thousands of enthusiastic spectators.

It was acclaimed as "one of the neatest and most commodious boat passages in Europe" but the company had spent four times as much on its associated new roads and the growth of railways made it unprofitable until the development of shipbuilding at Woolston from 1876 brought increased traffic.

Improved 'bridges' were provided, first of iron by Joseph Hodgkinson at the Crosshouse Iron Foundry, then in steel by Day, Summers & Co. at Northam — to use wire ropes instead of chains. The Northam-built No. 8 featured in the splendid riverside scene of about 1905 photographed for one of many attractive cards from the prolific French publisher Louis Levy (previous page). Built in 1896, it continued in service until 1961.

Some enterprising photographer got the crew of No. 7 to pose for another Edwardian card, issued by the London View Co. The overprint "Wishing You a Happy Birthday" may have helped to boost sales. No. 7, Northam-built in 1892, was denied the possibility of matching the 60+ years service records of Nos. 8 and 9 when it was sunk in mid-passage on March 8th, 1928.
Leaving the Southampton side on a dark and foggy afternoon, it was run into amidships by the tug *Fawley,* towing a laden barge down-river on a strong ebb tide. Small boats rushed to rescue all seventy passengers during the 15-20 minutes before No. 7 sank in mid-stream.

It was later dragged to the Woolston side and raised a few weeks later, sold off to serve as a pontoon at the nearby Supermarine works until broken up about 1940.

The floating bridges were used for pleasure trips as well as workaday journeys but the Royal Pier was the most popular place for townsfolk wishing to enjoy a breath of sea air without boarding a ship.

The pier was built in 1833 to provide landing stages for the early steamers but its recreational aspect soon complemented its original function, becoming greater after the development of the docks from the 1840s and the later extensions to the Town Quay. As reconstructed and enlarged in 1892, the pier offered a 780 ft. promenade, with refreshment facilities, alcoves, glass screens and seats, while at the pier head was a large and ornate pavillion used for military band and other concerts, dances and assorted entertainments. In the 1890s it was noteworthy that "the pier is lighted throughout with electric light"; the Harbour Board proudly advertised it as "one of the largest and finest piers in the south of England."

"Pier Toll 1d. Each" was the notice above the uniformed collector standing beside the turnstiles at the left of this picture — which must have been taken on a working day when promenaders were much fewer than at weekends.

This card of about 1905 was one of the Milton "Artlette" series from London publishers Woolstone Bros., who issued numerous "novelty" cards. Printed in Saxony, it was embellished with lines of stuck-on tinsel glitter — hand-applied in the days when cheap labour for such tasks was plentiful.

Woodmill, Southampton

Sept 12/04

THE MAYFLOWER MEMORIAL, SOUTHAMPTON.
THE UNVEILING CEREMONY BY DR HINES PAGE, THE AMERICAN AMBASSADOR, AUGUST 15th, 1913.

This Stuart card, sent to a schoolboy collector in 1904, presents an almost idyllic picture of Woodmill. It was then a corn mill, rebuilt after a fire in 1820, but earlier there was indeed a woodmill, where machines mass-produced vast numbers of standardised blocks for rigging and gun tackles aboard naval vessels.

Walter Taylor (1734-1803) was an inventive Southampton carpenter who — first with his father of the same name (died 1762) and then on his own — devised machine tools (some steam-powered) for sawing, boring and turning block components with hitherto unknown speed and accuracy. He also developed circular saws and improved pumps.

Beginning in the 1750s at premises in Westgate and Bugle Streets, Taylor transferred his operations in the 1770s to a new mill near Weston Lane: about 1782 he removed to Woodmill, to expand his business further. He also set up block-making factories on the Thames and at Plymouth and employed sub-contractors. Taylor received large sums from the Admiralty for his blocks, on which he held a virtual monopoly until losing his lucrative contracts in 1803.

His pioneering contribution was later overshadowed by the improved techniques of Marc Brunel, adoped at Portsmouth Dockyard — after Taylor declined Brunel's offer of collaboration.

An anonymous postcard photographer caught the moment when a canvas screen slid down to unveil the Mayflower Memorial on the afternoon of August 15th, 1913. Instead of cutting the release cord, the U.S. Ambassador, Dr. Walter Hines Page, burned through it with a silver "torch of liberty" presented by the local organising committee.

It originally proposed an elaborate representation of the *Mayflower*'s bow projecting over the water's edge but could not raise the required £2,000 and had to settle for a simpler — but still impressive — column, costing only £500.

Paucity of subscriptions was disappointing, for Southampton had a special claim to commemorate the "Pilgrim Fathers"; the West Quay was their original point of embarkation on August 15th, 1620, whereas their better-known association with Plymouth as their final port of departure was both incidental and accidental.

The religious exiles from Holland brought the 60 ton *Speedwell* to carry 30 of them to meet at Southampton with the *Mayflower* chartered from London, thrice her size and complement. The leaking condition of the former obliged them to put in for repairs, first at Dartmouth, then at Plymouth, where 102 of the original 120 pioneers (including the Southampton cooper John Alden) crammed aboard the *Mayflower,* leaving the *Speedwell* to be sold off. They finally set sail for America on September 16th.

A VIEW ON THE ITCHEN. FLOATING BRIDGE.

"Northam Toll Bridge 1800" is the crudely lettered caption on this anonymous Edwardian postcard reproduction of Philip Brannon's engraving, originally published in 1850. In the foreground, a sailing collier is shown discharging its cargo at a coal wharf.

The first timber bridge across the Itchen was built in 1797-99 for a company set up by local men with commercial and landed interests, to extend Southampton's communications eastwards − complemented by a similar Bursledon Bridge project; many subscribed to both.

The "spirit of improvement" then prevailing in the expanding town and the growth of its shipping trade also found expression in the Southampton-Salisbury canal scheme of the 1790s, although this proved short-lived and abortive, never serving "the great depot for coals at Northam", as intended by its promoters.

The 1796 Act authorising Northam Bridge envisaged a 25 ft. central drawbridge to allow passage of vessels to and from Woodmill, but this requirement was withdrawn in 1798.

The original timber bridge was replaced by a wrought iron one in 1889. Acquired and freed of tolls in 1929 by Southampton Corporation, this was superseded in 1954 by the present prestressed concrete bridge.

The Itchen Floating Bridge Company was compulsorily purchased by the corporation in 1934, by which time this form of ferry was becoming an anachronism, as vehicle traffic exceeded its capacity. Following incorporation of Woolston, Sholing and Bitterne into the borough in 1920, its replacement by a fixed road bridge was much discussed but not until 1977 did the new high-level City-financed Itchen bridge finally supersede the floating bridges − after 141 years.

The delicately framed, glazed sepia photograph on this Bealing card captured the scene eighty years ago, when traffic was less hectic but the Itchen was busier, with sailing vessels bringing coal, timber, cement and much else. Being steam-powered, the floating bridges were liable to delay as they followed proper etiquette in giving way to sail − not without some near misses!

In the late 18th century, as coastal trade expanded, the construction of private wharfs along the Itchen at Chapel and Northam had led to disputes between their owners and the corporation about non-payment of the "petty customs" due on goods landed at the town quays. These were resolved by the creation in 1803 of a board of Harbour Commissioners having overall responsibility for port development.

13 SOUTHAMPTON. — The Pier. — The Cowes Boat. — LL.

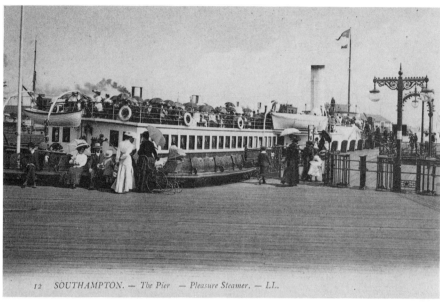

12 SOUTHAMPTON. — The Pier — Pleasure Steamer. — LL.

The Harbour Commissioners soon removed most of the old Watergate at the foot of the High Street to improve access to the Town Quay and in 1810 auctioned off the historic West Quay, but growth of steamship traffic in the 1820s caused increasing congestion on the main Town Quay. Although paddle steamers were not sufficiently well-engined and designed to run regular year-round services until the 1830s, even by 1830 it was claimed that 100,000 steamship passengers were annually passing through Southampton.

While it was still enjoying patronage as a residential resort, this expanding traffic enhanced its standing as a maritime centre, already a gateway to the Continent, a decade ahead of the advent of the railway and the first docks. These developments were reflected in the growth of the town from under 8,000 inhabitants in 1801 to over 27,000 in 1841.

The Harbour Board effected some improvements to the Town Quay but increased use highlighted its inadequacies. Steamship passengers often had to be conveyed from ship to shore in small boats or carried the final stage across the foreshore mud, then thread their way through piles of goods, ropes, barrows and wagons.

Steamship operators pressed strongly for better landing facilities, which the Harbour Board provided by borrowing the £10,000 needed to erect a substantial timber pier, running out to deep water. Opened with great ceremony on July 8th, 1833 by the Duchess of Kent and her daughter Princess (soon to be Queen) Victoria, it was proudly styled the Royal Victoria Pier, later simply the Royal Pier.

Within a few years its timber piles were badly affected by marine borers, which necessitated new foundations, scupper-nailed for protection. These served until a major reconstruction and enlargement was undertaken in 1890 — to the design of Edward Cooper Poole, the Harbour Board engineer and architect from 1887, when he took over the job from his father, whom he had previously assisted.

His new pier, officially opened by the Duke of Connaught in June 1892, was acclaimed the largest of its kind in the south of England, covering 3½ acres. Branching off the pierhead, flanking the handsome large pavilion, were landing stages for ten steamers, available at all states of tide for Isle of Wight services, excursion steamers and goods and livestock traffic.

These Edwardian scenes of passengers boarding the Cowes boat and a pleasure steamer were photographed about 1905 for postcards published for the English market by Louis Levy.

Landing Stage   Southampton

All arrived safely. Beautiful weather. Much love from all — Lawson.

Stengel & Co. Dresden-Berlin. 14482

2 SOUTHAMPTON. — View on Pier. — LL.

As steamer traffic grew, the Harbour Board provided a pontoon to supplement the facilities of the Royal Pier in 1866. Landing stages were increased to ten in number when the pier was enlarged in 1892.

This card emanated from Stengel & Co., a large German firm which produced thousands of different view cards for many countries — including Japan and Australia. From 1901 they were distributed in Britain by a London agent. The card illustrated was printed before half the back could be used for correspondence, hence the succinct message written on the front in the only space available.

The notice-board in the foreground welcomes arrivals with the announcement "New Grand Theatre, Southampton — open every evening with a first-class London company: Frequent Matinees", above a pasted-up display of its advertising bills.

Behind can be seen the impressive six-storey block of "Geddes Warehouse", completed in 1866 and still surviving — although now renovated to serve a very different purpose, as luxury flats and a restaurant (see page 60).

This L.L. card of the early 1900s caught the scene at the Royal Pier station, as a train and a line of horse cabs awaited the arrival of an Isle of Wight steamer.

To the right of the open door of the first carriage, beside the canopy advertising the gold medal mineral waters of Randall, Sloper & Co. (perhaps sold at the lemonade and ginger beer stall in the foreground), can be discerned the destination board for Waterloo.

The horse tramway from the Terminus station along Canute Road to the Town Quay, laid in 1847, was extended to the Royal Pier in 1871. Railway working was introduced in 1876, with five or six trains a day providing a through service for Isle of Wight travellers. Trains ceased using the timber-built railway terminus on the Pier in 1914, when its condition had so deteriorated that repairs were considered uneconomic — they might have cost £6,000!

Printed in France, this card was sent to Paris in 1908 through Southampton Docks post office, going for a halfpenny as printed matter, without any message or sender's name and with the stamp rather oddly stuck on the picture side.

The 1830s saw the start of the railway and docks developments which together provided the basis for Southampton becoming a major port. From the start, they were recognised as interdependent, each seen as generating traffic to promote the other's growth.

Both were originally proposed to be built by the same company, the Southampton and London Railway and Dock Co., authorised by Parliament in 1834. In the event, it was unable to enlist sufficient financial support and had to abandon its dock scheme — leaving that to be undertaken by a separate company established late in 1835.

Work started that year on the railway from Southampton to London, via Winchester, Basingstoke and Woking. From May 1838 it was opened in sections, with the whole length completed in May 1840. The London terminus was initially at Nine Elms, Battersea, until replaced by Waterloo in 1848 — when the best trains accomplished the journey in two hours.

The company — re-styled London and South Western Railway because of its extended interests — had a keen eye to the future. Its line into Southampton ran through 'suburbs' then largely open country, with its terminus sited east of the old town in an area still semi-rural but well placed in relation to the proposed docks.

Southampton's 1840 Terminus Station was intended to be impressive! Its architect, Sir William Tite, gave it a handsome stucco frontage in restrained classical style, making a splendid sight at the end of Oxford Street. Now 'listed', preserved and renovated for other purposes, it is one of Britain's oldest surviving railway buildings, with its exterior remaining essentially as designed a century and a half ago.

Ironically, it escaped modernisation because of the decline in docks traffic and the routing of most main-line services through Southampton West/Central station.

In 1858 its name was changed to Southampton Docks, becoming Southampton Town and Docks in 1896. The photograph at the left was presumably taken before then, although the postcard version was not issued until some years later. In 1923 the station was redesignated "Southampton Terminus (for Docks)". It closed in 1966 and its once busy platforms were turned over to car parking.

Southampton West station, photographed about 1900 for this Stuart card — which highlights the pre-reclamation extent of open water beyond it — was newly built in 1895. It replaced the original Blechynden station, initially a minor feature of the Dorchester line opened in 1847: extended and re-named Southampton West End in 1858, this was sited nearer the mouth of the tunnel.

Southampton West was enlarged and improved in 1935, when it was re-styled Southampton Central. After the closure of the Terminus station, it became simply "Southampton" in 1967, by which time rebuilding had involved demolition of the long-familiar clock tower.

COSSER, PHOTO;
SOUTHAMTPON.

The Docks, Southampton.

The docks, which typified Southampton for both residents and visitors, were frequently depicted on Edwardian postcards, as in this photograph by Whitfield Cosser, originally issued about 1902 and subsequently reproduced on several other cards; and another published anonymously not long afterwards.

Since the Harbour Board itself lacked the resources for the task, their construction was undertaken by the London-based Southampton Dock Company. It looked to the area east of the Town Quay and in 1836 persuaded the Borough Council (newly reformed and now more enterprising and representative of the town's business interests) to sell it 216 acres of mudlands — for £5,000. The laying of the dock's foundation stone on October 12th, 1838 was marked by elaborate ceremonies, witnessed by some 20,000 people — showing that the significance of the occasion was then widely recognised.

Although not officially opened until a year later, the 16 acre Outer Dock was first used on August 29th, 1842 by two ships of the Peninsular and Oriental company, which had come to Southampton in 1840, after securing the mail contracts indicated by its name. Its vessels were able to discharge cargoes direct into London-bound wagons, for the railway line had already been extended into the docks, although initially the motive power was provided by horses.

The P & O was soon followed by the Royal Mail company, holding mail contracts for the West Indies and the Americas. It selected Southampton as its headquarters on the basis of an engineer's report that "as a steam boat station it is unrivalled in England." Subsequent developments fully justified John Smeaton's assessment.

In the 1850s the Union Steamship Company became the third mainstay of the port, carrying troops and supplies to the Crimea and extending into the South African trade with a mail contract. North German Lloyd and Hamburg-America steamers began calling at Southampton in 1857-8, to be followed by other European lines, while the port also gained impetus from emigrant traffic to America and Australia, raising it to fifth place in the Kingdom, although then with only a tenth of the trade of Liverpool.

In line with this expansion, the Dock Company had constructed three dry docks in 1846-54 and the ten acre Inner (tidal) Dock, opened in 1851 and enlarged and deepened a few years later. In the 1870s facilities were further extended by the building of the Itchen Quays and a fourth dry dock (for Union Line vessels) but dock expansion nevertheless lagged behind the needs of the constantly increasing size and number of steamers using the port — a situation highlighted by the withdrawal of P & O services to London in 1881.

The Empress Dock, Southampton

Southampton's ambitions as "the Liverpool of the South" were tempered by the economics of early steamships, which emphasised more profitable passenger trade and specialist rather than bulk cargoes. Offsetting its own lack of industry and distance from the main manufacturing areas were Southampton's natural tidal advantages and convenient location in relation to major French and German ports as well as to London, particularly the short railway journey for liner passengers.

It therefore developed primarily as a base and port of call for mail packets and passenger steamers. Shipping, docks and associated port activities created many jobs and also promoted the town's 'service economy'. Reflecting this growth, the population of the borough increased from under 28,000 in 1841 to over 60,000 in 1881. Incorporation of the expanding suburbs of Shirley, Freemantle and Bitterne Park in 1895 boosted the 1901 census figure to 105,000; further growth and the 1920 boundary extension east of the Itchen carried the total to over 162,000 in 1921.

Shipping interests powerfully influenced the life and affairs of the town. Its Chamber of Commerce was set up in 1851 specifically to advance the claims of the port. Both Conservatives and Liberals sought leading men of the shipping companies to represent Southampton in Parliament. MPs included the co-founder of the P & O, Brodie McGee Willcox (from 1847 until his death in 1862); Russell Gurney of Royal Mail; Alfred Giles and F.H. Evans of the Union company.

Railway and dock companies had a general community of interest in the expansion of traffic and facilities for mutual benefit. The LSWR was itself closely involved in the docks scene, with 20 miles of track there by the Nineties and numerous wagons carrying cargo and coal — of which steamers then required vast quantities. It also ran steamer services to the Channel Islands and France (from the 1840s through a subsidiary company, from 1862 in its own right) which proved a profitable and expanding business.

Upkeep and improvement of facilities to cater for larger and larger liners strained the resources of the Dock Company, which was obliged to negotiate a loan of £330,000 from the LSWR to construct a new, much-needed, deep water dock. This 18½ acre development, providing 3,750 ft. of additional quay, was styled the Empress Dock, opened by Queen Victoria herself on July 26th, 1890. It enabled Southampton alone to accommodate the largest and deepest-laden ships of the day at any state of the tide. Later, it was associated with the port's extensive fruit trade and with overseas troop movements.

Scenes at the Empress Dock in the early 1900s are shown on these cards — the first issued by F.G.O. Stuart, the second by a national publisher identified only by his "W" insignia. The latter caught some smart Edwardian folk in front of ships of the Royal Mail, American and Union Castle lines.

Ocean Docks Southampton

17 SOUTHAMPTON — Ocean Quay. — L.L.

In 1892 the Dock Company was taken over (at a purchase price of £1.36 million) by the LSWR, bringing docks and railway under the same ownership, as originally envisaged in 1831. Injecting new capital, the LSWR embarked on a big programme of modernisation and construction to expand the docks to their full potential. It extended the Itchen and Test quays and provided a fifth dry dock, the largest in the world at the time it was opened in 1895 by the Prince of Wales (later Edward VII), whose name it was given. A sixth dry dock, styled Trafalgar, again the world's largest (912 ft. long and 100 ft. wide), was completed in 1905, ceremonially opened on the centenary of the Battle of Trafalgar, October 21st.

In 1891 over 10,000 vessels, totalling 1.75 million tons, entered and left Southampton, which was used by a dozen major shipping lines. Although passengers could embark for almost anywhere in the world, Southampton was then a terminal only for services to South America, the West Indies and South Africa, until in 1893 the American Line transferred its New York service from Liverpool to make Southampton its European terminal. The LSWR put on special Saturday morning boat trains from London and re-timed its Le Havre service as a feeder for New York sailings.

In 1894 Southampton became the principal centre for troop movements around the far-flung Empire. Within five years of the LSWR take-over the docks traffic almost doubled.

Southampton gained more traffic when the London-based Castle Line moved to the port in 1898 and the following year merged with its old rival, the Union company, to form the Union-Castle Line. More shipping companies came to Southampton, which could claim to be the country's premier passenger port after the White Star Line transferred its prestigious North Atlantic service from Liverpool in 1907. That same year Harland & Wolff opened ship repairing works in the docks.

To cater for liners now exceeding 40,000 tons, another large dock was needed. Giving 3,800 more feet of quay, this was completed in 1911. It was originally called the White Star Dock but renamed Ocean Dock in 1922, by which time almost all the major transatlantic services were based at Southampton, including the Cunard Line (another move from Liverpool) and Canadian Pacific from 1919-23. By 1914 Southampton was handling three times the volume of shipping it had in 1891 — an index of the success of LSWR investment and promotion.

Liners in the Ocean Dock (including the *St. Paul* at the right) featured on the anonymous card illustrated at the left. A workaday scene on the Ocean Quay — the docks were then largely unmechanised for cargo handling — appears on this Louis Levy card; the photograph was probably taken about 1906, although the card was not used until 1922.

While screw propulsion superseded paddle power for ocean-going steamships, paddle steamers long remained in favour for coastal services, ferries and excursions; 'pleasure steamers' enjoyed great popularity.

At Southampton, their main operator, formed by merger in 1861, was the impressively named 'Southampton, Isle of Wight and South of England Royal Mail Steam Packet Company Ltd.' — probably the longest named of any British registered company but since the adoption of a uniform new livery in 1935 now more conveniently known as Red Funnel Steamers.

Through four decades until 1939, postcards provided cheap mementoes of trips aboard the company's vessels. Illustrated here are two of those published by E.J. Frampton of Bournemouth. They featured the company's insignia, listed its "fleet of pleasure steamers" and the places they served — excursions along the coast embracing Brighton and Weymouth and across the Channel to Cherbourg, as well as regular year-round services to the Isle of Wight.

Depicted on an early card of about 1900 is the *Solent Queen,* a two-funnelled steamer of 324 tons, Glasgow built in 1889. She survived being gutted by fire, off the Royal Pier, on April 27, 1893, and was back in service within three months after speedy repairs at Northam. Day, Summers & Co. repaired her again in 1906, following collision with a ferry steamer in Portsmouth harbour.

The *Solent Queen* maintained essential local services during both World Wars. Her dash to Dunkirk in 1940 sadly ended in return without being able to take off any troops. Having spent her last years altered to carry cars on the Cowes run, her career of nearly sixty years ended in 1948, when she was withdrawn and scrapped.

More elaborate and colourful cards were issued by Frampton from about 1904, probably produced abroad (his name was printed as Erampton). Typical of this series is the one featuring *Her Majesty,* a 325 ton paddler built at Glasgow in 1885.

She also had a varied career, lasting 55 years. She was raised and repaired by J.G. Fay at Northam after being sunk by the liner *Paris* in the Empress Dock on February 13, 1896. The American Line seems to have accepted responsibility for this accident.

Her Majesty served as a minesweeper in 1917-19, then resumed regular passenger services to Cowes until 1927, when she was converted to carry about 18 cars. She also carried cargo and from 1935 served as a tender to the *Normandie* and other big liners calling at Southampton.

Her Majesty was sunk during the German air raid of December 1, 1940, while lying off Platform Wharf at the company's repair jetty. She was later raised and broken up.

14 SOUTHAMPTON. — *The Pier, the Balmoral.* — LL.

22 SOUTHAMPTON. — *S. S. Lorna Doone.* — LL.

The ubiquitous Louis Levy also had a keen eye to the market for cards of pleasure steamers. Here is one of about 1905 showing the *Balmoral* at the Royal Pier.

Built in 1900, this 473 tonner was the largest and fastest of the company's fleet, its flagship until 1939. Ordered to compete with P.A. Campbell's *Cambria,* she was a steel ship, with five watertight compartments, able to carry a thousand passengers who could enjoy the facility of a full-length promenade deck and thrill as she made 19-20 knots.

Captain A. Goldsmith was her well-liked master from 1906 until his retirement in 1938. The *Balmoral* ran long day trips from Southampton and Bournemouth, frequently to Cherbourg. Her profitability depended on good summer trade, for she was regularly laid up for nearly three quarters of the year.

She was requisitioned early in 1915 as a troop transport, later converted for minesweeping duty. After the war, she was reconditioned and returned to excursion work in 1921, continuing until World War II, when she became an auxiliary anti-aircraft ship, afterwards an accommodation vessel on the Clyde.

When returned, the *Balmoral* was no longer fit for economic reconditioning, so she went for scrap in 1949.

"This is the steamer which plies between Southampton and Bournemouth during the summer via the Isle of Wight" wrote Cecil from Southampton in 1907, sending to fellow collector Malcolm this L.L. card of the *Lorna Doone.*

This highly popular 427 ton pleasure steamer was built on the Clyde in 1891 for a Cardiff company running trips to Ilfracombe — hence her naming for the heroine of R.D. Blackmore's Exmoor novel, which was retained after the Southampton company acquired her in 1898.

Alterations gave her a full length promenade deck and her elegant accommodation included a bar styled "Half Way Doone" and a lounge called "The Retreat" — features which perhaps enhanced her appeal to the excursionists who flocked aboard her year after year. Her master for most of the years 1900-28 was Captain G. Jenman, who claimed on his retirement that "there is no man living who has been round the Isle of Wight more than I have."

The elaborate gold leaf scroll work on her paddle box gave way to Admiralty grey in 1914, when the *Lorna Doone* was requisitioned as a patrol boat, then converted to a minesweeper. Operating as part of the Dover patrol, she survived German air attacks, shelling, floating mines and being run into.

After a further 20 years more peaceful service, she was again requisitioned in 1939 for naval duty, first as a minesweeper, then as an accommodation ship. This time she returned in poor condition, to be laid up and scrapped.

7 HYTHE (near Southampton). — The Pier. — LL.

"I have chartered the Hythe steamer to convey my Xmas greetings to you all" wrote the sender of this Mentor card – posted to his friends in Shirley on December 23rd, 1905, doubtless in confident expectation of next-day delivery.

Two sturdy paddle steamers then operated the service between Hythe Pier and the Town Quay. Built at Plymouth in 1887, the *Hotspur* (first of six to carry that name, adopted in compliment to the Percy family interest in the ferry company) was a 62 tonner able to carry 200 passengers. She lasted 40 years, until replaced in 1927. Failing to find a buyer, she was stripped and left to rot at Dibden Bay.

The *Hotspur* was complemented by the *Hampton* (featured in the postcard photograph), a similar vessel built by Day, Summers & Co. at Northam in 1894. She did duty even longer, becoming the last of the paddlers on the Hythe Passage, finally withdrawn in 1936 and sold to Dutch breakers.

The Hythe ferry, offering a passage much preferred to the 12 mile land route in the days before good roads and motor transport, was noted on a map of 1575 but for centuries earlier local boatmen must have rowed or sailed their wherries to and from Southampton, carrying assorted cargoes and passengers.

From 1830 paddle steamers competed with them but successive operators provided only intermittent services and there were landing problems at Hythe, even after a stone quay or hard was constructed in 1845. Plans for a 2,000 ft. iron pier, with a pontoon, were brought to fruition in 1880, at a cost of £7,700. Dry landing facilities greatly enhanced the ferry traffic and the pier also attracted New Forest excursionists, anglers and others who enjoyed watching the larger shipping scene.

In later years the 'Queens' often drew large crowds to the pier, which was also heavily strained with spectators on July 8th, 1952, when the *United States* made her maiden arrival at Southampton.

The pier was replanked in 1896. Tramlines were laid along it in 1909, used for hand-propelled luggage trolleys until electric locomotives and passenger carriages were introduced in 1922.

An Edwardian view of Hythe Pier, with the *Hotspur* alongside it, is given on this L.L. card, posted on Christmas Eve 1907 to send seasonal greetings to Birmingham. Even in 1907, it was perhaps too much to hope for Christmas Day delivery there!

The Town Quay, Southampton

WILLSTEED.   REDBRIDGE QUAY.

Originally a small landing place outside the old Watergate, the Town Quay was marginally extended with a jetty built piecemeal by the corporation in the 17th and 18th centuries. The Gas Column was erected on the Town Quay in 1829 to serve as a 'seamark' but it was removed as an obstruction in 1865 and transferred to Houndwell.

After effecting various small-scale improvements, the Harbour Board undertook a series of sizeable extensions from 1853, building warehouses and providing more berths for smaller cargo vessels. In the days before road haulage, coastal shipping carried great quantities and variety of goods: to handle some of them, one of the world's first electric wharf cranes was in service on the Town Quay from 1893.

The Town Quay reached its present shape in the late 1890s, as shown on this card issued a few years later by the major publishers Valentine & Co. of Dundee.

The horse-operated tramway of 1847 to the Terminus station became a railway line in the 1870s, while by 1900 vehicle access from the west was improved by a new road along the Western Shore. In changed conditions, when traffic had diminished, freight train services to the Town Quay were withdrawn in 1970.

This Edwardian photograph of Redbridge Quay, issued as a postcard by Herbert Willsteed, gives a reminder of the extent to which, in the early years of this century, small coastal vessels carried substantial amounts of cargo to little ports and jetties all round the country. Sailing ships traded mainly in bulk cargoes like coal, timber and building materials, while Redbridge provided the basis for further ship-borne traffic in its railway sleeper and concrete works and the local production of chemical fertilisers.

Important as a crossing place at the head of the Test estuary, with a history dating back to Saxon days, Redbridge later became a busy maritime village, whence New Forest timber was shipped to Portsmouth and where a score of wooden warships were built by various contractors to supplement the output of royal dockyards during times of war, in the 1690s, 1790s and 1810s.

In 1796-8 Redbridge was chosen by Samuel Bentham, inspector general of naval works, as the site for building six experimental vessels to his own design and supervision, intended to show how 'men of war' could be constructed using far less timber than hitherto — for reasons of forest conservation. The master shipwrights involved, Hobbs and Hellyear, continued building merchant ships at Redbridge until 1825.

The Andover-Redbridge canal, opened in 1794, brought wharf trade to Redbridge but this fell away after its closure in 1859. Branches off this waterway were the basis for the abortive Southampton and Salisbury canal of 1803-08.

The LSWR gave Southampton its first 'grand hotel', a handsome five-storey building in High Victorian style abutting the Terminus Station. Originally the Imperial Hotel, started in 1865 by a private developer who soon went into liquidation, it was acquired and completed by the railway company, which re-named it South-Western Hotel in 1871. It flourished as the fashionable stop-over for well-to-do railway and steamer passengers and the base for visiting VIPs. With a 7-8 storey extension in the Twenties, it enjoyed its heyday between the wars, catering for the rich and famous. Requisitioned in 1939, it never re-opened and was converted to accommodate the BBC and Cunard offices.

Now a 'listed building', the hotel is here depicted on a postcard issued about 1920 by Short and Millard, who ran a photographic business in Commercial Road. Besides the horse-drawn delivery van of George Dawe Ltd (with its advertisement for Bourneville Cocoa) this also shows — on the tower at top right — the mast and "time ball" operated there from 1904 as a joint service by the LSWR and Harbour Board to give a reliable visual signal for checking ships' chronometers. On an electrical impulse from Greenwich, the ball (5 ft. in diameter) dropped down at exactly 10 a.m. daily, until the arrangement was discontinued at the end of 1933, when radio time signals made it superfluous.

From its inception in 1888 until 1903, the time ball operated (at 1 p.m.) on the tower of what was then generally called the Old Prison or South Castle i.e. God's House Tower — since 1960 the city's archaeological museum. This medieval artillery tower housed various categories of prisoners in the 18th and 19th centuries but from 1875 the corporation leased the buildings to the Harbour Board as stores.

This W.H. Smith card shows the door of the gallery lettered as "Ice Store" (sub-let to the ice merchant Austin Gough), while the former time ball mast now serves to fly the advertising banner of the other tenant for thirty years from 1905 — Holzapfels Composition Co. Ltd. Its office sent the card on July 1st, 1908 to a Bournemouth builder advising "have despatched the 2x1 galls Ivory White enamel per Pickfords carr. paid."

This was small stuff for the company which by the time it opened its Southampton branch in 1905 had already built up a world-wide chain of subsidiaries and depots to supply its special compositions for preventing marine fouling and corrosion of ships' bottoms. This extensive business was started on Tyneside in 1881 by Charles Petrie and the German brothers Max and Albert Holzapfel. In 1918, when it moved its headquarters to London, the company changed its name to International Paints and Compositions Co. Ltd. — later shortened to International Paint.

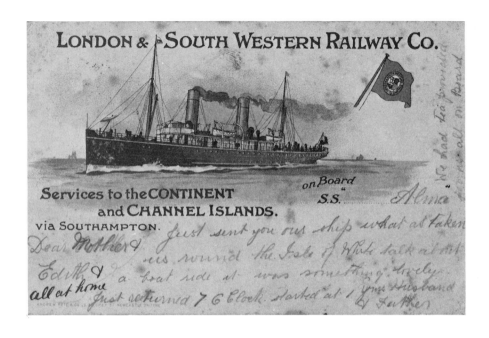

"Just sent you our ship what as taken us round the Isle of White talk about a boat ride it was something lovely. Just returned 7 o'clock, started at 1. We had tea provided for us all on Board". On August 3rd, 1904 "Your Husband & Father" sent this message to "Dear Mother, Edith and all at home" on a Hampshire farm, using one of the cards sold − or perhaps given away − to excursionists on the LSWR steamer *Alma*.

A late patriotic naming for the Crimean War battle, she was then just ten years old, a steel vessel of 1,145 tons, built on Clydebank, along with her sister-ship *Columbia*. Until sold out of the railway fleet in 1912, they were notable for their tall and widely spaced funnels − and for being the first vessels to provide separate cabins for passengers on its Southampton-Le Havre services.

"Holiday Tours" as well as "services by mail steamers to Havre (for Paris), Cherbourg, St. Malo & Channel Islands" were advertised in a panel on the address side of the card, leaving only part of the front for correspondence. The 1904 writer may not have been the best scholar produced by a Board School but he was typical of many such people: expansion of public education from the 1870s created a mass market for postcards among those whose level of literacy might often have inhibited them from writing more formally by letter ... at twice the postage cost.

The LSWR ordered its multi purpose 'on board' cards from the Newcastle firm of Andrew Reid & Co., which specialised in shipping and railway cards, mostly lithographed in Germany. Artistic and colourful, such cards were often kept as souvenirs of holiday trips, later surfacing from old albums to delight present-day collectors.

They are complemented by photographic cards such as this view of four LSWR steamers in the Outer Docks, issued by Valentine & Sons of Dundee, one of the most prolific and wide-ranging postcard publishers.

In the foreground is the long-lived *South Western*. Built on the Thames in 1874, she ran mostly to St. Malo and remained in service for 44 years until torpedoed in 1918. Beyond her are the sister-ships *Alma* and *Columbia* − confusingly double-berthed − and another railway steamer at the far right, not now identifiable. The buildings along the far quay are the site of today's Ocean Village.

Although the photograph was taken some years earlier, this card was still available for use in October 1914, when it was sent (without benefit of censor) to Gert at Salisbury by her friend who wrote "just a few lines to tell you that we got safe to Southampton and we go tonight but we don't know what time ... I am alright and we are leaving for the front, so that is all xxxx" Let's hope it was not literally that for him and his girl ...

THE R.M.S.P. COY'S S.S. "MAGDALENA" LEAVING SOUTHAMPTON.
TONNAGE 5,370

BEKEN
COWES

R. M. S. "Orinoco"

F.G.O. Stuart. 56

In December 1839 the young Queen Victoria signed the charter setting up the Royal Mail Steam Packet Company, which then began a Southampton connection continuing unbroken until 1971. In December 1841 its first three vessels left the port to take up station in what was to become a comprehensive mail and passenger network embracing North and South America, centred around the West Indies, its most complex part. Over the next 120 years the company was to prosper, decline, be taken over and re-emerge in a different form, before finally ending in anonymity as part of a Chinese-owned maritime empire.

The elegant Royal Mail liner *Magdalena* leaving Southampton is featured on this Edwardian card, in a fine photograph by Frank Beken of Cowes, the pioneer yachting and marine specialist whose second and third generation family firm has long enjoyed international renown throughout the nautical world.

The *Magdalena* is the vessel immortalised in Kipling's poem "Armadilloes":
"I've never sailed the Amazon,
I've never reached Brazil;
But the *Don* and *Magdalena*,
They can go there when they will.
Yes, weekly from Southampton,
Great steamers white and gold
Go rolling down to Rio ---"

The RMS *Orinoco* is the subject of this F.G.O. Stuart card, one of his earliest, issued about 1903. Like the *Magdalena*, she was the product of Clyde shipbuilders in the late Victorian age, when sailing ships were outliving their commercial function but had reached their most beautiful form, transferred to the steamers which were superseding them. The *Orinoco* (1886, 4,434 gross tons) and the *Magdalena* (1889, 5,362 tons) spent most of their working lives on the Royal Mail's West Indies routes.

The *Orinoco* was the Royal Mail's first steel ship, the first to be fitted with electric light and the last square-rigged vessel built for the company. The *Magdalena* was the last ship to have square sails but by the time these postcard photographs were taken both vessels had lost all evidence of their earlier sailing connections.

Still to be seen are their old open canvas-protected bridges — which must have presented some uncomfortable experiences for deck crews in even moderate Atlantic winds. On sunny days in the Solent, however, the shipping scene was greatly enhanced by the appearance of these graceful yacht-like vessels.

This early Stuart card, posted at Southampton in September 1902, offers a striking — and now quite rare — view of the *Danube*. In 1901 the Royal Mail had most of its vessels given white hulls and upperworks, with buff funnels. However, in the age of coal, it was soon found that such elegance was both impractical and expensive to maintain, so 1903 saw them revert to black hulls, while retaining their buff funnel colours.

Whatever their colour scheme, the *Danube* was typical of several small but well proportioned vessels built for the company in the late Victorian times. Launched on the Clyde in 1893, she was a single screw steamer of 5,946 gross tons, developing a speed of 15 knots from her four boilers and 32 furnaces.

Her passenger capacity was 215 first, 36 second and 350 third class; most of the latter would have been emigrants or migrant workers headed for South America.

The *Danube* made the first of 107 voyages to South America from Southampton in January 1894. After serving as a troopship in 1915-18, she was sold out of the Royal Mail fleet in 1920. Renamed *Mediterranean Star*, she was evidently not successful, as she was scrapped in 1922.

Ocean liners generated vast and increasing quantities of laundry — sheets, pillow-cases, table cloths, napkins, crew's uniforms and other items. There were limits to what could be handled on board, so much of it awaited change-over in port, shuttled off in wicker baskets to and from laundries in Southampton, some on contract, others run by the shipping companies themselves.

From 1900 until it transferred to the docks about 1920, the "Royal Mail Steam Packet Company's Washing Establishment" — to give it its full directory title — occupied premises at Old Shirley, off Romsey Road, that had previously been a brewery and earlier a mill of great antiquity, using the head of water from the confluence of Hollybrook and Tanners Brook.

The Royal Mail laundry staff posed for this picture one day in the early 1900s. The card was produced anonymously and uncaptioned but it has been identified by an elderly lady who worked for Royal Mail as a girl. Its blurred postmark date probably 1909, it was used by a Southampton lad whose message to a friend in Winchester had nothing to do with the laundry — although he may have been one of the two young men in the picture, wearing their caps for the camera in proper Edwardian fashion.

Impressively making something like her full speed of 17 knots is the *Arlanza*, depicted on this photographic card issued by Kirk of Cowes — which indicates well enough why the Royal Mail management did not long persevere with white hulls for its steamships.

The *Arlanza*, built in 1911 by Harland & Wolff at Belfast, was a vessel of 15,044 tons, 590 ft. overall, with a 242 ft. promenade deck. Five hatches served her sizeable capacity for refrigerated cargo. She made her maiden voyage to the River Plate in September 1912 and left Southampton for the last time on her final voyage to the same destination in 1938.

At the start of World War I the *Arlanza* featured in an interesting incident involving the *Kaiser Wilhelm Der Grosse* (page 30). The German liner, then fitted out as a raider, captured her off the Brazilian coast — but released her when her passengers were found to include many women and children. Such old-fashioned gallantry harked back to earlier notions of naval warfare, soon to be forgotten as the war at sea intensified and German vessels engaged in unrestricted sinking of merchantmen.

Later, the *Arlanza* herself became an armed merchant cruiser, enjoying a fortunate escape when mined off northern Russia. Her crew and owners must have greeted the Armistice with great relief.

"Dear Ethel — Just a photo of the ship, love. It goes on Thursday. I thought it was Wednesday but I have to be on board at 8 a.m. on Thursday. Hope you will like it. We have rotten weather here. I am pleased to have got that ship as it is the only sort of life which I am used to but I don't suppose I shall always do it. The ship is going to the West Indies and Caribbean sea and will take 42 days. Love to all at home, your affectionate brother George."

Postcard messages from passengers or visitors have survived in much greater numbers than those from crew members, such as this. It was pencilled on the back of this anonymous sepia "real photograph" card depicting the Royal Mail liner *Avon* passing the Itchen Quays as she left Southampton. George sent it in an envelope and did not put the date but he probably wrote not long after the vessel was built in 1907.

She was one on the nine so-called "A" ships ordered by Royal Mail and delivered between 1905 and 1914. At over 11,000 tons, the *Avon* was considerably larger than any previous company ships, representing part of the Royal Mail's effort to update and reinvigorate itself during these years.

She operated between Southampton and South America for most of her career but also ran cruises to Norway and between New York and Bermuda at various times, besides serving as an armed merchant cruiser during World War I. The *Avon* was broken up in 1930.

KAISER WILHELM DER GROSSE PAQUEBOT ALLEMAGNE

S. S. "Deutschland" in Dry Dock, Southampton.

German transatlantic lines began their Southampton connections in 1857, when Norddeutscher Lloyd (NDL) steamships on their Bremen-New York run first called at the port. The Hamburg American Line (HAPAG) followed a year later. It quitted Southampton in 1869 but returned in 1889; thereafter, the companies moderated their rivalry by making alternate Wednesday calls.

From 1840 to 1897, except for six years, British vessels were almost unchallenged holders of the "Blue Riband" for the fastest Atlantic crossings. In 1897 the NDL's grandly named *Kaiser Wilhelm Der Grosse* (here depicted on a French postcard) first wrested the coveted (albeit notional) trophy for Germany, which retained it for ten years.

The maiden voyage of the *KWDG*, calling at Southampton on September 20th, 1897, excited intense public interest. That day, wrote one maritime journalist, "I had the opportunity of going down from London by the passengers' special train to have a look at her. The start was an early one and the train was heavy, for a large number of passengers were booked by her. We reached Southampton at 11 a.m. . . . It was announced that the tender would go out at 2.30. As it reached Netley, the liner's four funnels appeared upon our starboard bow and very soon the ship dashed up, passed us, and anchored off the Hospital. Meanwhile, there was a tremendous amount of cheering, band playing and waving of handkerchiefs."

The admiring Southampton crowds were seeing what has been called "the first true modern luxury ocean liner" − not only fast but at 14,349 tons then the world's largest passenger ship. Built at the Vulcan yard in Stettin (now Szczecin in Poland), she was sleek and rakish, with two pairs of buff funnels (rather than just four of them) and a fine counter stern, all combining to give the impression of power and speed typical of a pre-1914 breed of German vessels.

On her third voyage in November 1897, the *KWDG* did the 3,605 mile Atlantic run from Sandy Hook to the Needles at an average 22.35 knots and continued to achieve high speeds enhancing the reputation of NDL in the Atlantic trade. Not until 1907 was she outpaced by the *Mauretania*.

Her great rival was the *Deutschland*, here shown in dry dock at Southampton on one of Boots "Pelham Series" cards. Also built at Stettin, in HAPAG service from 1900, she was larger (16,700 tons) and marginally faster but excessive vibration and mechanical troubles disappointed Albert Ballin's high hopes. HAPAG had to run her at less than her planned speed, renaming her *Victoria Luise* in 1911 and using her for cruising. Later, as the *Hansa*, she made a few Atlantic voyages in 1922-24 before being scrapped.

The *KWDG* had been built with a strengthened deck as a potential naval auxiliary cruiser but she fell an early victim of the war, sunk off the coast of West Africa by HMS *Highflyer* on August 27th, 1914.

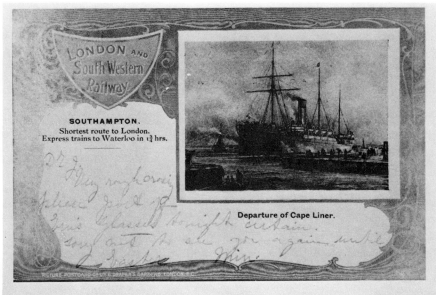

Departure of Cape Liner.

For generations of Southampton ship-watchers, perhaps the most appealing sights were the lilac-hulled vessels of the Union-Castle Line. That distinctive colour, complemented by white superstructure and red and black funnels, made the company's ships look most attractive and elegant, whether berthed at the end of the Itchen Quay (34-6) or, later, at berths 101-2 in the Western Docks, prior to departure for the Cape.

This Stuart card shows a group of Union-Castle liners off the Ocean Quay about 1905.

The company resulted from the merger in 1900 of the competing Union and Castle Lines. Arthur Anderson, co-founder of P&O, was the leading spirit in starting the Union Steamship Co. in 1853. It began with colliers, which it chartered to the government for troop transport and supply duties during the Crimean War, then secured the mail contract for South Africa. This was inaugurated on September 15th, 1857, when the tiny *Dane*, 530 tons, left Southampton on her 44-day voyage to the Cape with the mails — and six passengers.

The Castle Line, founded five years later by Sir Donald Currie, was based on London and did not make regular calls at Southampton until 1891. From 1876 the two companies shared the South African mail contract on an alternate week basis, until merger ended their rivalry.

This rare card is typical of those produced in 1899 by the short-lived Picture Postcard Co. Ltd. of London, which found a specialist outlet in supplying advertising cards to several railway companies, including the LSWR. Such cards may have been given away or sold (ready-stamped) from vending machines at railway stations.

They were of distinctive size, half an inch each way less than the standard 5.5 × 3.5 inch "continental" format, which was not authorised by the GPO for domestic use until November 1899. These advertising cards offered neat sepia or black and white vignettes of scenes in the area served by each railway company, set in a coloured ornamental surround containing its name and related text.

In the case of Southampton, the message was clear — "Shortest route to London: Express trains to Waterloo in 1¾ hrs" flanked a picture "Departure of Cape Liner." The artist probably did not intend to depict a specific vessel but, with rigging and spars on the foremast, it might derive from the *Tantallon Castle* or *Dunvegan Castle*, both just over 5,500 tons, built in 1894-96. Neither lasted long in company service, being almost outdated at the time of construction.

Only a small space on the front of the card was available for correspondence. This one was used in August 1903 from Southampton to Newport, Isle of Wight, with the message "Very rough crossing. Please post off Ern's glasses tonight certain. Sorry not to see you again until Easter." Was Ern off to South Africa? Did he get his specs before he sailed?

My dear Lawrence,
Thank you very much
for your nice letter;
it was beautifully
written.
This is the ship that
General De Wet
went back to the
Cape of Good hope in.
With love from
L. Harris.

Nov. 9th 1902.

15 SOUTHAMPTON. — Durham Castle. — LL.

One of the fascinations of collecting old postcards is coming across one with a message that takes you right back to the time it was published. This card, one of the first issued by F.G.O. Stuart in 1902, was used in November that year, sent to a schoolboy in London. Confined to the space beside its picture of the Union liner *Saxon* (see page 39), the writer complimented Lawrence on his "nice letter . . . beautifully written" and added "This is the ship that General De Wet went back to the Cape of Good Hope in."

Although on the 'wrong' side, Christian De Wet was a character in true 'Boy's Own' mould, big game hunter and author as well as redoubtable Boer leader, a master of sudden raiding attacks and ambushes who inspired widespread guerrilla warfare against the British forces — most of whom were carried to South Africa on troopships leaving Southampton.

The Boer Wars of 1899-1902 divided British opinion from the outset but even ardent imperialists showed real sympathy for the game losers after they signed a peace agreement on May 31st, 1902. In August, the defeated Boer generals De Wet, Botha and De La Rey were received with generous cheers, almost as heroes, when they landed at Southampton, on a mission to London to seek more aid for rebuilding and re-stocking Boer farms. They had to return home empty-handed but their departure from Southampton did not pass unnoticed.

Most publishers of shipping postcards liked to show a good side profile of a ship, placed in the centre of the photograph or painting and often set against a dramatic or familiar background. Louis Levy, the Paris publisher who issued so many distinctive cards, wanted something different, such as this fine shot of the Union-Castle liner *Durham Castle* tied up at a Southampton quay one balmy Edwardian day, about 1907.

Superb photography and printing enables you to see clear details of her deck gear, derricks and hull construction, also the canvas-covered open bridge — not a popular place on a cold or stormy day: and have you spotted the funnel of a tug peeping up at her bow?

The composition is enhanced by the people in the foreground; a group of dock workers, idle for a moment, gaze at the passing lady, carrying her parasol as she trails her skirts between the railway tracks, and gentlemen in smart suits and boaters. Another man seems to have stopped to take a closer look at the liner.

The *Durham Castle* (1904-40) was termed an 'intermediate' liner, one of those serving a longer route, calling at various ports up the east coast of Africa.

The sober-suited staff − all male − of a Southampton shipping office posed for this photograph, issued anonymously as a postcard, some time just before or just after World War I. Well in evidence are the high bench desks at which serious-looking clerks worked on their hefty ledgers. Passenger and cargo traffic alike involved extensive paperwork, all meticulously hand-recorded. This sort of labour-intensive office scene continued little changed from Edwardian times into the Twenties and Thirties.

This office must have been typical of several of its kind, probably one of the larger shipping companies like P&O, Union-Castle, Cunard or White Star, all established in Canute Road, or Royal Mail, with its headquarters in Terminus Terrace.

There were, of course, many other shipping companies, large and small, with offices and agents in Southampton during the early decades of this century. Besides the major German, Dutch and American lines, they included Elder, Dempster & Co., the Red Star Line, several Liverpool and other coastal cargo companies, Scottish and Irish shipping firms, not forgetting the LSWR steamers.

From Southampton, you could then travel, or despatch goods, almost literally to any port in the world . . . there was always some company or agent waiting to serve you.

Competition between rival shipping companies, whether running transatlantic passenger liners or small coastal carriers, was often acute − price-cutting wars are nothing new − but this did not exclude cameraderie among their port staffs. Specialisation in different shipping routes assisted friendly relations between the old-established lines whose business interests did not directly conflict, as in the case of Royal Mail, which concentrated on services to South America and the West Indies, and Union-Castle, running mainly to South Africa.

Before World War I, the offices of these two companies combined to field a football team. It does not seem to have played in any local league and lack of reports in Southampton newspapers suggests its matches were of no great consequence − perhaps mostly against sides from other shipping offices? Nevertheless, the U-C and RMSP footballers of 1913 were a well turned out lot, who commissioned this professional postcard photograph.

It carries the imprint "A. Rapp, Marine photographer, 39 Bernard Street, Southampton." Adolphe Rapp was first listed at that address in 1908 as a "foreign bookseller" but he soon diversified into photography. He found a useful sideline in taking shots of football crowds at the Dell and teams like this. Rapp moved to Bridge Street about 1914 but did not stay there long.

U.S.M.S.S. "NEW YORK"
PASSING NETLEY HOSPITAL.

IN THE DOCKS, SOUTHAMPTON.

"Please excuse this p.c. It is the only one I can find" wrote a Southampton lady on January 6th, 1910, telling another "I have returned home and shall be glad to know when next there is any hockey." The drawing of the *New York* passing Netley Hospital is not particularly well done and the card was cheaply produced, evidently for company publicity purposes. Presumably, supplies were available aboard the liner, on which the sender had been a passenger.

The card is significant, for when the American Line inaugurated its New York-Southampton service in 1893 it made an important contribution to Southampton maritime history, sealing a connection of fame and fortune between the two ports that lasted until the Fifties.

The *New York* began service in 1888 as the British built and flagged *City of New York*, a 10,499 ton steel, twin screw vessel, which could then be claimed the world's largest, since Brunel's 18,915 ton *Great Eastern* of 1860 was then about to be broken up. Initially operated from Liverpool by the Inman & International Company, she was transferred to American registry in 1892, the year the company secured the U.S. mail contract having Southampton as its terminal. Along with her sister *City of Paris*, she was then acquired by the American Line, which dropped "City of" from the liners' names.

The *New York* first arrived at Southampton on March 4th, 1893 and a week later sailed for New York on what soon became a weekly service, involving three other vessels. By 1897 the American Line was carrying more first and second class passengers than any other line. In 1898 service was briefly interrupted when four liners were chartered by the U.S. Government for use as armed cruisers during the Spanish-American War; the *New York* (temporarily renamed *Harvard*) returned to commercial service within the year.

The American Line was now part of the International Navigation Company, which grew into a vast organisation, controlling many different lines, re-styled the International Mercantile Marine Co. in 1902. That year her owners had the *New York* re-engined, with her original three funnels reduced to two, as shown on this postcard photograph of her in Southampton docks, published by Whitfield Cosser & Co., of Southampton and Salisbury, around 1905.

By then the *New York* had been joined by more modern vessels, including ships of other companies within the complex IMM organisation. In 1914 the New York-Southampton services were diverted to Liverpool; when the United States entered the war in 1917, the *New York* was commissioned as a troop transport, *USS Plattsburg*. She resumed service from Southampton in February 1920 but that November she was withdrawn. Sold to the Polish Navigation Co., she made only two more transatlantic voyages before being scrapped in 1923.

32 SOUTHAMPTON — S. S. Saint-Louis. — LL.

The American Line's *St. Louis* and her sister ship *St. Paul* (page 46), both built in 1895 at Cramp's Yard in Philadelphia, were very much nineteenth century liners. With their three masts, low superstructure, tall funnels and counter stern, they had an elegance that was lost over the next decade in the rush to build bigger and better.

Of 11,629 tons, 535 ft. long, with a service speed of 19 knots, the *St. Louis* was built to carry 350 first, 200 second and 800 third class passengers. In 1913, when she was already 18 years old and no longer heading the luxury ratings, her accommodation was redesignated to provide only second and third class passengers.

The family photographed beside the gangway at Southampton docks on December 10th, 1913, en route to New York aboard her, were presumably content to travel second, prosperous though they appeared! This unposted anonymous card must have surfaced from some old family album; it was evidently produced as a one-off personal souvenir, probably by an enterprising 'quick print' photographer who snapped passengers as they were about to board and delivered the cards before they sailed.

Such cards, processed to order in small batches, were one of the staples of the 'Golden Age' of postcards — catering for folk who liked to send visual evidence of particular experiences or occasions or the house they lived in, not without an element of oneupmanship!

Issued some years earlier, the French origin of this card, another in Louis Levy's extensive Southampton series, is reflected in its caption "S.S. Saint-Louis." Well past her prime, the liner became of declining importance to her controlling company, which literally had other lines in the water. In the early 1900s the American business tycoon J. Pierpoint Morgan, one of the great 'Robber Barons', powerfully extended his interests into shipping; his IMM company acquired effective control of the American, White Star, Dominion, Leyland and Holland-America lines, as well as having agreements with the German NDL and HAPAG companies.

In 1914, the *St. Louis*, like other transatlantic liners, was switched from Southampton to Liverpool. With the entry of the United States into the war in 1917, she was taken over as a troopship, renamed *Louisville*. This was her second wartime commission; back in 1898 she had served, with name unchanged, as an armed cruiser during the Spanish-American War.

The intended return of the *St. Louis* to her former transatlantic duties in 1920 did not materialise; she suffered severe fire damage while refitting and was sold out of the American Line fleet. Nothing came of her new owners' plans to turn her into an exhibition ship. The American Line itself was phased out, ending operations in 1923, the year the *St. Louis* and her sister *St. Paul* were towed to Europe for breaking up.

Following the takeover of the White Star Line by the International Mercantile Marine Company, the decision to transfer its prestigious transatlantic service from Liverpool in 1907 ensured the dominance of Southampton as a passenger port.

The White Star Line had been built up from the 1870s by Thomas Ismay, with the backing of the Belfast shipbuilders Harland & Wolff. It became the pride and showpiece of the IMM group, which undertook an ambitious building programme. In 1907 large crowds gathered at the Empress Dock to watch the arrival of the Belfast-built *Adriatic* (subject of another fine Stuart card), which on June 5th inaugurated the White Star's Southampton-New York service.

Reviving the name of one of the line's first steamers (1872-99), she was over six times its size, a big vessel of 24,541 tons. In their day, the *Adriatic* and her consorts *Celtic*, *Cedric* and *Baltic* were known as 'The Big Four'. To cater for the increasingly large passenger liners of the time, the LSWR invested in further dock capacity, opening in 1911 what was initially called the White Star Dock, later the Ocean Dock.

In 1911 the *Adriatic* resumed sailings from Liverpool. She returned to Southampton in 1919-22, then reverted to Liverpool-New York services until sold in 1934 to Japanese breakers.

Although overshadowed by her sister ship the *Titanic*, the White Star Liner *Olympic* has her own place in maritime history and a career not without incident – four times she hit or was hit by other vessels. When she made her maiden voyage to New York from Southampton on June 14th, 1911, she ranked as the world's largest liner. Built by Harland & Wolff, she could carry 1,054 first, 510 second and 1,020 third class passengers, with a crew of 65 deck officers, 320 engine room staff, and 475 catering personnel.

In the aftermath of the *Titanic* disaster, she underwent the first of three major refits. This involved a complete new inner skin; her first class accommodation was reduced by 25% and her tonnage was increased from 45,324 to 46,359 – as given on this Hoffmann card, first issued in 1924 and often reprinted. The aftermost of her four funnels was a dummy.

After serving as a troopship from 1917, the *Olympic* returned to Southampton in 1920, remaining a familiar sight in the port until her last commercial voyage in March 1935, following which she went for scrap.

She was unlucky in her intended consorts. Besides the *Titanic*, the even larger *Britannic*, completed in 1915, was sunk by a mine in 1916 – in the Aegean, whilst serving as a hospital ship: she never ran in White Star colours. In the inter-war years, the *Olympic* was more fortunate in her partners, the ex-German vessels *Homeric* and *Majestic*.

1193 C. R. Hoffmann,
Southampton.

R.M.S. OLYMPIC   Length 900 Ft.   Breadth 99 Ft.   46,359 Tons
FIRST CLASS VERANDAH CAFE.

DAMAGE TO WHITE STAR R.M.S. OLYMPIC after collision with H.M.S. HAWKE
SEPT 20, 1911

The best size, shape and distribution of accommodation for a successful ocean liner were matters of debate. The huge pre-1914 German vessels did not all enjoy good reputations; liners built primarily for speed were prone to disconcerting vibration and were not wholly comfortable in mid-Atlantic conditions.

The White Star management eschewed speed and concentrated on passenger comfort. To many, the *Olympic* seemed to have got everything right. She was certainly well appointed, one of the first 'floating palaces', with a profusion of public rooms remarkable for their spaciousness and variety of styles. First class passengers had a Louis Quinze lounge and a Jacobean dining room and while gentlemen took their after-dinner brandy and cigars in the Georgian smoking room, their ladies could retire for coffee and liquors in the elegant Verandah Cafe — cups and glasses can be seen on the tables in this photograph, issued as a Hoffmann card in the late Twenties.

Luxury and elegance had to give way to mass catering in 1917 when the *Olympic* was taken over as a troopship, ferrying thousands of men across the Atlantic. In the English Channel on May 12th, 1918 she was involved in an unusual action; she rammed and sank the German U 103 after narrowly evading one of its torpedoes. Earlier, in 1914, the *Olympic* had distinguished herself by attempting to tow into port the battleship HMS *Audacious*, damaged after striking an enemy mine.

Three months after her maiden voyage, the *Olympic* was in collision in the Solent with cruiser HMS *Hawke*, which sliced into her on September 20th, 1911 — in full daylight and on a calm sea. The 7,300 ton cruiser's bow tore a large hole in the liner's starboard side near the stern, affecting several second class cabins. Fortunately, they were all empty, since the passengers were taking lunch at the time, and there were no casualties on either vessel.

The *Olympic* limped back to Southampton, while HMS *Hawke* was taken to dry dock at Portsmouth. This photograph of the damaged liner, issued as an anonymous postcard, was presumably taken soon after she had reached the quayside, as a number of passengers, mostly female, can be seen looking over her side, as workmen survey the gash below. The *Olympic* had to proceed to Belfast for repairs, missing a scheduled voyage.

An official enquiry later held the White Star Line to blame, because of the powerful suction exerted by its vessel. Seven months later, the same force from her sister ship the *Titanic* dragged the *New York* from her moorings as she left the quay to start her ill-fated maiden voyage. The story is told that one American passenger from the *Olympic* that September afternoon in 1911 was so anxious to get home that he dropped through the hole in the liner's side, into a small boat which he hired to take him ashore so that he could get to Liverpool and catch another White Star liner bound for New York.

Atlantic Hotel, Southampton

Up to 1914, millions of emigrants, travelling steerage or third class, constituted the 'bread and butter' traffic of most shipping lines. In 1894, to cater for the many folk passing through Southampton to start new lives overseas, John Doling opened his "Emigrants' Home" in Albert Road. Within a few years, this expanded into a large 4-storey block, styled the Atlantic Hotel from 1908. It was featured on his publicity postcards, which also showed the polyglot notices of the adjoining shop, where Eli Loftus traded from 1902 as outfitter and money changer.

The card illustrated here was sent to a mother in London to say "This is a photo of where we are living. I have 3 suits, 15 ties, 2 dozen collars, 3 hats, 1 pair boots, 5 shirts and sundry other articles — and don't forget the bicycle etc. Complete we are!" It was posted on August 5th, 1914 — the day after war was declared. Did the sender get away before emigration stopped for the 'duration'?

Certainly, the war put an end to the Atlantic Hotel and the Loftus business. Occupied by the British American Tobacco Co. from 1916 and damaged by fire in 1922, from 1930 the building housed a Ministry of Labour employment exchange for seamen. Refurbished, it is now suites of offices.

Cornish 'Cousin Jacks' were celebrated for their enterprise in seeking new opportunities abroad to apply their mining, engineering and other skills. For forty years until the mid-Thirties, those emigrating through Southampton could stay at their own "Cornish Hotel" in Orchard Place near the docks.

Shown on this 1920 photographic card, this private temperance hotel was run by the firm of Fairburn, Martin and Fleet. Perhaps two of the partners are the men standing outside the hotel entrances, beside shipping company posters and notices "General Passenger Agents — Book Here for Canada, America, South Africa & All Parts of the World."

Fairburn, Martin and Fleet gave up running their hotel in 1934. The premises were taken over by Mr. R. P. Bolestridge but his "Cornish Cafe" and "Cornish Boarding House" closed after a couple of years — presumably for lack of customers, whereas previously the hotel in Orchard Place had been a 'home from home' for men like the one who sent this card home on August 14th, 1920. He wrote "This is the Hotel we put up at, quite a nice place. Some crowd of people going across — one feels quite at home here among so many Cornish folks, and a nice lot of them too.'

Arrival of the Royal Mail Steamer "Scot"

S.S. SAXON passing the NEEDLES.

The main port of destination for Union-Castle liners was Capetown ; they thus became known affectionately as "the Cape boats." One of their earlier number was the elegant Scot, pictured here at Capetown, in a colourful quayside scene of bustle and excitement, with horse transport plentifully in evidence.

Her bowsprit and yacht-like bow are seen to full advantage, also her figurehead of Sir William Wallace; out of sight was her equally attractive counter stern, which gave her a clipper-like appearance, enhanced by her hull being painted white, with fawn upperworks and cream funnels.

Like her sailing ship forebears, the Scot was fast. On her first voyage from Southampton in July 1891 she knocked a whole day off her rivals' times. In 1893 she set a record for journey time to the Cape which lasted over forty years — 14 days, 18 hours and 57 minutes. Speed was expensive, however : despite her popularity with passengers, she proved a loss-maker and was withdrawn in 1903.

The back of this splendidly coloured card bears the imprint "Printed in Saxony" and the letters "St. & Co., B," which identify it was produced by the Berlin firm of Stengel & Co. Its Dresden printing works turned out some 30 million cards a year and by 1901 the company offered 10,000 different view cards covering most parts of the world.

This card reproduces a painting by the marine artist Neville Cumming showing the Saxon passing the Needles. The Saxon, of 12,385 tons, built by Harland & Wolff at Belfast, was the last vessel ordered by the Union company.

Delivered after its merger with the Castle line, she kept her original name but took the colours and house flag of the newly created Union-Castle line, which became so familiar to Southampton over the ensuing 77 years.

The Union-Castle house flag was first flown from the masthead of the Dunnottar Castle, leaving Southampton on March 17th, 1900.

The Saxon, carrying up to 600 passengers, served the South African route for 29 years and after that lay at Netley Buoys, still on call as a reserve ship, until 1935, when she went to the breakers.

This Edwardian picture of the Saxon was one of a set of six (No. 9133) reproductions of Cumming paintings of Union-Castle vessels in the "Celebrated Liners" series forming part of the extensive range of "Oilette" cards inaugurated in 1903 by Raphael Tuck & Sons. For four decades from 1900 the vast output of this London firm — proudly proclaimed as "Art Publishers to Their Majesties the King & Queen" — gave it the leading position among postcard publishers. It specialised in reproductions of paintings by notable artists — printed in England, not abroad.

S. S. Kaiser Wilhelm II.
F. G. O. Stuart. 1557

S. S. "Kaiserin Auguste Victoria" Hamburg—America—Line
F. G. O. Stuart. 1321

"Saw this ship off this morning, as well as the White Star liner *Oceanic,* West Indian packet *Oruba* and the NDL *Bülow"* was the message written on November 10th, 1909 by the sender of this fine Stuart card.

The most impressive sight of his morning's ship-watching was its subject, the *Kaiser Wilhelm II,* one of the largest liners then afloat. Named for the then popular 'Kaiser Bill' - whose imperial yacht was a familiar Edwardian sight in the Solent — she was a regular caller at Southampton on NDL service from 1903.

Another product of the Vulcan yard at Stettin, she carried forward the style of her predecessors (page 30) on a larger scale — 19,361 tons, with a passenger capacity of 775 first, 343 second and 770 third class. Her maiden voyage in April 1903 included a call at Southampton, as did her many others across the Atlantic. She took the Blue Riband for westward and eastward crossings in 1903 and 1906, running many other fast trips until 1914, when the outbreak of war found her at New York, where she was interned.

In 1917 she was taken over by the American government and converted into a troopship, called the *Agamemnon.* In 1927 she was renamed *Monticello* but then did little more than rust away at anchor. In 1940 she was in too poor a state even for Britain to accept the offer of her, despite urgent wartime shipping needs, and so she went for scrap.

Although built in the same Stettin yard, the *Kaiserin Auguste Victoria* — subject of another Stuart card printed in Germany — was very different from most of her Teutonic contemporaries. After unhappy experience with the *Deutschland,* HAPAG had her built for comfort rather than speed. She was named after the Kaiser's mother, who was a daughter of Queen Victoria.

This 24,600 ton liner, in service from 1906, put the emphasis on luxury, boasting suites with private bathrooms, electric lifts, a winter garden and medicinal baths. Such facilities were not, of course, for the bulk of her passengers — 1,820 in third class and steerage. Hamburg was a great transit port for emigrants to the 'New World'; German lines took the lion's share of this movement, profitably combining 'quantity' and 'quality' in their transatlantic traffic.

Having remained inactive at Hamburg through the war, the *KAV,* like most other HAPAG liners, was taken by the Allies under reparations arrangements. For a year she ran transatlantic services for Cunard, before being bought by Canadian Pacific in 1921, given a major overhaul and converted to oil, to be renamed *Empress of Scotland.*

She made her maiden voyage as such from Southampton to New York in January 1922 and then inaugurated a new service to Quebec. Ironically, she made Hamburg her European terminal. Her Canadian Pacific career ended in 1930, when she was withdrawn for scrapping.

Cosser, Photo;
Southampton. The Western Esplanade Southampton.

WESTERN ESPLANADE, SOUTHAMPTON. No 2038

This Cosser photograph enjoyed an unusually wide postcard circulation, not only through successive editions of his own card but also by its reproduction in various styles on at least a dozen others, issued up to 1917 by different publishers, both national and local.

His camera caught the scene on the Western Esplanade not long after its central feature was unveiled at a civic ceremony on July 27th, 1901. Designed by Herbert Bryans, this neat canopied Portland stone structure, whose columns surround a drinking fountain (itself disused since 1939) is usually called the *Stella* memorial but it was erected by public subscription specifically in tribute to the selfless devotion shown by Mrs. Mary Ann Rogers, senior stewardess of the LSWR steamer bound from Southampton to Guernsey, in calmly helping passengers during the fatal few minutes on the afternoon of Good Friday, March 30th, 1889, after the *Stella* struck a rock off the notorious Casquets, 8 miles west of Alderney, and sank almost immediately, with the loss of nearly half the 200 people aboard.

One of three sister ships built on the Clyde in 1890 for the LSWR, she was a single funnelled twin-screw steamer of 1,059 gross tons, a popular vessel on the Southampton-Channel Islands service.

Despite running into heavy fog, Captain Reeks (who went down with his ship) seems to have continued at full speed, probably mindful of the competing GWR steamer *Ibex* from Weymouth, scheduled to reach Guernsey at the same time.

There were often unofficial 'races' between steamers of the rival railway companies on this prestigious service, until the Board of Trade enquiry into the *Stella* disaster led their managements to adopt different timings for their Channel Islands sailings.

A relief fund helped the widows and dependents of the *Stella* victims; charitable ladies "who had been kindly tended by Mrs. Rogers on passages to Guernsey" organised a separate appeal to help her aged father and orphaned children (she worked for the LSWR to support them after her husband had drowned in the company's service in 1883) and erect a memorial to her. Its initiator, Miss Frances Power Cobbs of North Wales, was responsible for the long inscription on the bronze plaque fixed to its central pillar.

This records that "amid the confusion and terror of shipwreck, she aided all the women under her charge to quit the vessel in safety, giving her own lifebelt to one who was unprotected. Urged by the sailors to make good her escape, she refused lest she might endanger the heavily laden boat. Cheering the departing crew with a friendly cry of "Goodbye, goodbye", she was seen a few minutes later, as the *Stella* went down, lifting her arms upwards with the prayer "Lord have me", then sank in the waters with the sinking ship."

"Actions such as these . . . constitute the glorious heritage of our British race. They deserve perpetual commemoration because . . . they recall to us forever the nobility and love-worthiness of human nature."

The Stuart card (bottom left) shows a more general view of the area; easily recognisable today except for the cannon and the intact Royal Pier.

"This is rather a sad postcard but I thought you would like to have it" wrote Fred to Eliza in December 1905. "It is the remains of our steamer *Hilda* that was wrecked last month. It is marked and autographed by the only British survivor. The × is where he hung on for 12 hours until our other boat came out and saw them. We have had a trying time in the office over it. There were five French peasants saved besides Grinter. I knew the captain and officers very well."

Fred must have worked in the LSWR office at Southampton docks. The company's iron screw steamer *Hilda*, Glasgow-built in 1882, had made hundreds of crossings on its Southampton-St. Malo run. Her commander for over 15 years was Captain Gregory, who had a house in Tennyson Road, Portswood; all the ship's crew lived in and around Southampton, including James Grinter, then in his fifties, father of a large family, whose home was in Frederick Street, Newtown.

On the night of November 18th, 1905, the *Hilda* was engulfed in a fierce snowstorm and raging winds, which dashed her on the rocks near St. Malo. She healed over and sank within minutes, breaking in two: it was impossible to launch any of her boats.

Grinter later described his ordeal — "People were swept away all around me. I found myself clinging to the mainmast, which I climbed, and stretching myself out I clung dazed and stupified at the thought of all the lives lost in a few minutes. I don't know how the hours passed but I just held on tightly to the mast while the snow seemed to freeze on my face."

Grinter marked on the card where the Chief Mate clung for hours until he dropped off to his death, also the line of rigging on which five hardy Bretons survived for twelve hours until they and Grinter were seen and rescued next morning by a boat from the *Hilda*'s sister ship *Ada*, heading out of St. Malo. It seems the lamp at the *Hilda*'s masthead remained alight, shedding a little life-saving warmth on those below it. The death toll was 27 crew and 100 passengers, mostly Breton onion-sellers returning from their annual visits to England.

The six survivors were afterwards photographed (Grinter being the trim-bearded man at the left) for another of the series of cards devoted to the *Hilda* shipwreck by the St. Malo publishers "Collection Germain." Captioned in both French and English (not without some misprints!), they went through several different editions.

James Grinter doubtless received some modest recompense for autographing cards for well-wishers. Understandably, he never returned to sea but found a job with the Customs in Southampton docks. He lived on into his eighties, dying in 1953.

"Raising the S.Y. EROS by the Western Marine Salvage Co. in Southampton Water, Sept. 22nd, 1907" is the caption on the back of this topical card from F.G.O. Stuart, quickly produced in black and white by his British printer to record an operation which attracted considerable interest as "a difficult task smartly performed."

The *Eros* was a 770 ton luxury steam yacht, built on the Thames in 1885 for Baron de Rothschild and acquired in 1907 by the Liverpool shipowner and M.P. Robert Houston. He did not long enjoy voyages aboard her, for on the night of September 3rd, at anchor below Hythe Pier, she was run down by a Liverpool collier, the 2,635 ton *Knightsgarth*, outward bound from Southampton.

Her owner had earlier gone to London; his guests and the crew were quickly rescued by boats from other yachts and the *Knightsgarth*, before the *Eros* sank, with a 45 degree list to port in 20 ft. of water at low tide. Lloyds entrusted her recovery to a Penzance salvage firm, whose men lost little time in fitting wooden patches over her holes, pumping her out, getting her afloat and towing her to No. 1 Dry Dock, where Thornycrofts undertook repairs.

The collision mystified Southampton shipping correspondents, who could only speculate about "a breakdown in the *Knightsgarth*'s machinery or a derangement in her steering gear": her skipper was respected as a reliable and experienced man, "thoroughly conversant with the river" who had had no previous accidents. The night was calm and not particularly dark; both vessels had lights.

In May 1908 it was announced that the salvaged *Eros* had been sold to the British agent of the government of Liberia, to become a coastal patrol gunboat. She was converted by Summers and Payne in the Inner Dock. After going to Portsmouth to have guns fitted, the vessel returned to Southampton, to receive a civic send-off when she left for West Africa on October 5th, under the command of a seconded British naval officer.

She was renamed RLS *Lark*, reviving the name of a small British armed vessel which had constituted the original 'navy' of Liberia sixty years previously. With few roads through its undeveloped interior, the country depended largely on sea links between its coastal towns. The *Lark* did good service, helping to check smuggling and collect taxes, but was afterwards laid up to deteriorate until she sank off Monrovia about 1925.

In the days before 'flag of convenience' registrations nominally gave it one of the world's largest merchant fleets, the West African republic was proud of its single gunboat — literally a 'postage stamp navy', for from 1909 the *Lark* was depicted on several of its stamps; these colourful pictorials were once very popular with junior collectors.

S. S. Suevic. (12,500 tons gross.)

S.S. "SUEVIC" AT SOUTHAMPTON.

This card — one of the "Peacock Autochrom" series from a London publisher, colour printed in Saxony — was used to send seasonal greetings from Southampton to Winchester in December 1907. That year, the 12,500 ton White Star cargo and passenger steamer *Suevic* became the subject of many topical postcards, illustrating the remarkable saga of her wreck, salvage and reconstruction — during which she could be claimed the world's longest ship, with her stern at Southampton and her bow at Belfast!

Handed over in 1901, she was the last of five sister ships built by Harland and Wolff at Belfast to run the White Star's new monthly service to Australia. For six years, the *Suevic* enjoyed success and popularity in this service but on the night of March 17th, 1907, homeward bound from Sydney with 382 passengers and a large cargo, she ran into fog off the Lizard and, with her captain misjudging his course, drove hard on the rocks, where she remained firmly impaled.

Fortunately, there was no loss of life. Four Cornish lifeboats rescued all the 456 people aboard. The passengers, with most of their luggage safely brought ashore, were taken to Helston to catch trains to complete their journeys.

During the next few days much of the cargo — as diverse as frozen meat, wool, butter and rabbit skins — was taken off the *Suevic* by local vessels but efforts to refloat her proved fruitless. Captain Fred Young, in charge of operations by the Liverpool and Glasgow Salvage Association, then made the bold decision to cut in two the 550 ft. long steamer, around her second mast, since the after part, with passenger accommodation, engines and boilers, was undamaged.

Oxy-acetylene cutting was not then available, so the separation was effected by a series of small gelignite charges, carefully placed to sever the *Suevic* just aft of her bridge. This dangerous and delicate operation was successfully accomplished and the stern half (almost two thirds, in fact) was hauled off, leaving the damaged bow abandoned on the rocks. Early in April the stern section was towed to Southampton, steered by tugs but partly moving under its own steam.

Its arrival aroused great public interest. F.G.O. Stuart was among the photographers who hastened to take pictures of this strange-looking craft; he soon issued postcards that found a ready sale. Those showing the cut-off stern were followed by others depicting it in the Trafalgar dry dock, where repairs were put in hand, awaiting the construction of a replacement bow ordered from the ship's builders at Belfast.

S.S. "SUEVIC" IN DRY DOCK, SOUTHAMPTON.

TOWING NEW BOW OF S.S. "SUEVIC," BELFAST TO SOUTHAMPTON.

PHOTO BY BAIRD, BELFAST.

Harland and Wolff lost no time in getting a new 212 ft. bow section ready for delivery in October. It was built on a normal slipway but launched bow first to protect the bulkhead. Ballasted with machinery for the company's newly opened repair works in Southampton docks, it left Belfast on October 19th, 1907 for its six-day journey to Southampton.

This provided another highly photogenic subject for topical postcards, such as the one illustrated at the right, by Baird of Belfast. It was posted from Southampton on November 4th, with a note by the sender — "in tow of the tugs *Pathfinder*, (2 funnels) and *Blazer*. The bow is now in dry dock to be joined to the stern portion. It is a wonderful work. The *Suevic* is announced to sail on its regular service on January 17th."

The White Star management had in fact advertised the sailing of the reconstructed *Suevic* even before the new bow entered the water — such was their confidence in the precision of its builders and the craftsmanship of Thornycroft's repair department, which skilfully joined the two sections together in the Trafalgar dry dock. With a slight overlap on the salvaged section, the new bow was exactly fitted and secured, to complete the final phase of this remarkable feat of 'ship surgery'.

Ten months after her stranding off the Lizard, the 'good as new' *Suevic* returned to her Australian service. During World War I she was requisitioned for troop carrying and steamed a quarter of a million miles on government service. Resuming her Australian runs, after an extensive refit at Portsmouth, she went on to complete her fiftieth round trip, arriving at Southampton on March 14th, 1924 — having then covered 1.2 million miles in all.

The *Suevic* was eventually withdrawn from White Star service in 1928 and sold (for £35,000!) to a Norwegian company, who had her converted at Kiel to become the whale factory ship *Skytteren*.

She was interned at Gothenberg in April 1940. Two years later she was scuttled by her crew in the Skagerrak to avoid capture after being intercepted by German warships while trying to escape to Britain.

This time there was no question of salvage. The former *Suevic*, secure of her place in the history of maritime salvage and reconstruction, had ended her notable career extending over more than four decades.

35 R. M. S St-Paul leaving Southampton. — LL.

ST. PAUL IN DRY DOCK AFTER COLLISION WITH H.M.S. GLADIATOR. AP.25.08

In the early hours of Saturday, April 25th, 1908, an unexpected heavy snow storm blanketed the Southampton area to a depth of 2 ft., bringing the town to a virtual standstill. Enterprising photographers like Herbert Willsteed and George Courtney saw the commercial possibilities of such unseasonable snow scenes and slithered around with their cameras to take pictures for postcards which they quickly produced for topical sale. Many of these evidently went straight into albums, for examples are still plentiful.

Local photographers soon found another subject for their postcards in the aftermath of the collision which occurred in a blinding blizzard at 2.30 that afternoon. Off Yarmouth, the American Line's *St. Paul*, which had left Southampton for New York two hours earlier, ran into and sank the cruiser HMS *Gladiator*, en route from Portland to Portsmouth.

Pictured here leaving Southampton on a L.L. card bought in 1906, the 11,629 ton *St. Paul*, built at Philadelphia in 1895, was then one of the world's largest liners. History was made aboard her in November 1899 during her passage from New York to Southampton, when Marconi set up a receiver and established short-range, wireless telegraphy communication with a station at the Needles; the news items he received were circulated in a sheet styled "Transatlantic Times", the first of its kind.

In almost nil visibility that April afternoon in 1908, the *St. Paul* seems to have been making 16 knots when she came up against HMS *Gladiator*, a second class cruiser of 5,750 tons, which was proceeding more cautiously at about half that speed. The *St. Paul* struck her amidships on the starboard side, her bows penetrating deep into the cruiser's hull. When the liner backed off, the badly gashed cruiser flooded rapidly and started to keel over; she sank within 15 minutes. The *St. Paul* gave prompt assistance but 26 of the warship's company were drowned; only three bodies were ever found.

After rescuing survivors, the *St. Paul* was able to return to Southampton, where her passengers – who suffered nothing worse than shock – were accommodated to await the sailing of the White Star's *Teutonic* four days later. The *St. Paul* went into the Trafalgar dry dock for Harland and Wolff to repair her damaged bows. There she was photographed for this sepia postcard issued by G.D. Courtney; such cards provided a useful supplement to the counter trade of the chemist's shop he kept in Derby Road for 35 years up to 1939.

The *St. Paul* sailed again for New York on June 20th, 1908. By strange coincidence, she capsized at her berth in New York harbour on April 25th, 1918, exactly ten years after her collision with the *Gladiator*. She was salvaged and resumed transatlantic service in 1920-22 but in 1923 she went for scrapping in Germany.

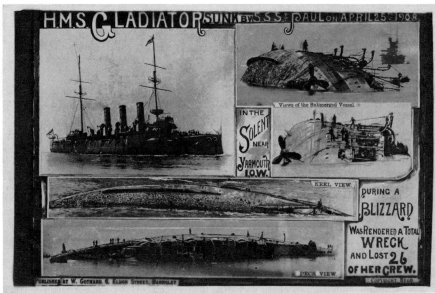

The wreck and subsequent salvage of the *Gladiator*, lying on her starboard side in low water 400 yards off the coast near Yarmouth pier, attracted many sightseers, as well as photographers like F.G.O. Stuart, who issued three cards showing the wreck.

Salvage operations – depicted on this card by Stephen Cribb of Portsmouth – were difficult, for the *Gladiator* had a 50 ft. gash along her submerged starboard side. Captain F.W. Young of the Liverpool Salvage Association was entrusted with the task of refloating her. He organised the removal of her armour, armour plating, funnels and ventilators, carefully sealing each hole. Then two tripods were erected on the port-side plating, with heavy wires leading off to powerful tugs. Seven 50 ft. pontoons were lashed alongside and 280 tons of iron were piled on the keel to serve as a counterweight.

Five months after she sank, the *Gladiator* was righted and towed to Portsmouth. The salvage work cost the Admiralty over £50,000: the wreck was sold to a ship-breaker for less than a third of that sum.

At a time when newspapers printed few illustrations and cinema news reels were in their infancy, there was a ready sale for photographic postcards documenting topical events, particularly disasters and 'human interest stories'.

The wreck of the *Gladiator* attracted the attention of one of the most enterprising and innovative publishers of such cards, established in the seemingly unlikely location of Barnsley. In 1908 the business of Warner Gothard, then run by his sons, was specialising in memorial cards, pioneering techniques of photo-montage to produce ingenious – albeit sometimes rather crude – compositions of unusual detail and interest. Most were devoted to mining and railway accidents and royal visits but they ranged widely in subject and place.

This is one of three featuring the wreck of the *Gladiator*, combining five pictures of her before and after sinking. Companion cards depicted the *St. Paul* and all 26 of the cruiser's crew lost in the collision: obtaining in short time portraits of so many dead men must have been quite a task.

Warner Gothard cards, which have not survived in great numbers, are now highly esteemed by collectors and much sought after as the classics of their kind.

The tragic story of the sinking of the *Titanic* on her maiden voyage from Southampton to New York in 1912 is too well known to need retelling here.

The second in the White Star trio of giant luxury liners, following the *Olympic* (pages 36-37) and intended to be complemented by the *Britannic*, the 46,329 ton *Titanic* was likewise built by Harland & Wolff at Belfast. Several Belfast publishers issued postcards showing her at various stages of construction and White Star company cards publicised her as "the largest steamer in the world."

After her arrival at Southampton on April 4th, 1912, local photographers like G.D. Courtney, H. Symes and H. Willsteed quickly produced postcard pictures of the latest shipbuilding marvel, which aroused great interest. Although the public were not allowed aboard her, thousands gathered to admire the *Titanic* at Berth 44 or take sightseeing steamer trips around her.

This Courtney card shows the liner leaving port on April 10th. The shadowy figure seated on a bollard in the foreground has been identified as Captain Steele, the White Star marine superintendent at Southampton. He faced problems organising coal supplies for the *Titanic*: a shortage in the aftermath of a miners' strike was met by transferring their remaining stocks from other White Star and American Line vessels temporarily laid up in the port.

Had the *Titanic* not been able to sail on time, perhaps she might have been spared colliding with an iceberg in the North Atlantic?

The departure of the *Titanic* at noon on April 10th was in fact delayed for an hour when the suction and turbulence created by her propellers dragged the *New York* (page 34) from her mooring at Berth 38: she swung dangerously close to the *Titanic* but the crew of the tug *Vulcan* managed to get a line aboard her.

Within a few days, the unbelievable had happened. As soon as news reached Southampton, the White Star offices in Canute Road were besieged by anxious crowds seeking news of their relatives. After agonising days of waiting and hoping, it was established that of the 1,316 passengers, 825 were lost, together with 673 of the crew of 885. Most of the latter were from the Southampton area, many with homes in Northam and Chapel, where whole streets were plunged into mourning and despair. Some 600 Southampton homes were stricken by the disaster.

The distress of bereaved dependents was somewhat relieved by a Mayor's 'Disaster Fund', to which Southampton folk contributed £48,482.

Many 'In Memoriam' postcards of the *Titanic* were produced throughout the country and several Southampton publishers featured the local memorials to the victims. Most prominent, in East Park, was the impressive granite and bronze tribute to the engineer officers, all 36 of whom remained at their posts and went down with their ship.

More modest was the Portland stone drinking fountain erected in memory of the crew (stewards, sailors and firemen). This card, issued by Rood Bros., wholesale stationers of Bevois Valley Road, shows it in its original position on the southern edge of the Common; it was moved in 1972 to the Merchant Navy memorial at Holy Rood church.

Raphael Tuck's "Celebrated Liners" series (see page 39) included a set of six (No. 9151) depicting Royal Mail steamships, of which this is a fine example. Neville Cumming's realistic painting shows the *Nile* leaving Southampton — against a Waterside background that in Edwardian times was still completely wooded, before any of the industrial and housing development so evident today.

The *Nile* was technically similar to the *Danube* (page 28) although at 5,855 tons she was slightly smaller than her sister ship. October 19th, 1893 saw her first departure for Rio and Buenos Aires — to which the first class single fare was then £35. In 1900 she did trooping duty to South Africa, as Transport No. 82, carrying 1,371 officers and men.

Returning at the end of that year, she continued in Royal Mail service until 1911, when she was sold to joint American-Hong Kong interests, to operate a service to San Francisco.

World War I brought another phase in the career of the *Nile*, which became a U.S. Navy transport in the Mediterranean and Indian waters. She afterwards returned to the Pacific but in 1922 she was laid up, to be scrapped three years later.

Another Royal Mail steamer, the *Aragon*, is shown here entering the Empress Dock. Unlike the "Oilettes", which were printed in England, this Tuck card (one of the Southampton "View" set No. 4794) was "processed in Holland" — colouring an originally black and white photograph. Until 1914, Continental, especially German, printers held the lead in colour lithography and many British publishers had their postcards printed abroad.

The *Aragon* was the first of the RMSP's 'A' class ships, representing a revolution in travel to South America. Built by Harland & Wolff at Belfast, of 9,588 gross tons, 513 ft. long, she was the Royal Mail's first twin screw vessel, larger and better appointed than any of her predecessors. She received much publicity — including three cruises in local waters for invited guests — before making her maiden voyage from Southampton on July 14th, 1905.

Her career was cut short during World War I. Requisitioned in 1914, she saw most of her service in the Mediterranean, notably in the ill-fated Dardanelles campaign. On December 30th, 1917, she was torpedoed off Alexandria. Despite efforts to save her and rescue the 2,700 men aboard her, the *Aragon* sank with loss of 610 lives.

Two very different cards depict two apparently very different ships — but really the same ship at different phases of her 37 year life.

The first card is an artistic composition, produced in the Twenties by Waterlow & Sons Ltd., the famous security printers better known as suppliers of postage stamps rather than postcards. It publicised the "Union-Castle Line Royal Mail Service to South & East Africa", with a glimpse of a "cabin-de-luxe" and an inset picture of the 19,023 ton *Arundel Castle* — aboard which such cards were doubtless available for passengers' use.

The company card shows the liner as built by Harland & Wolff in 1921. With her sister ship, the first *Windsor Castle,* she marked a considerable advance in the Union-Castle fleet. Half as big again as any of its previous vessels, the *Arundel Castle* was the company's first four-funnelled liner and its first to be propelled by geared turbines, which developed 17 knots.

Starting her maiden voyage from Southampton on April 22nd, 1921, her arrival in South Africa aroused great interest, heightened by the passenger list on her return trip including General Smuts and members of his government, travelling to England for an Imperial Conference.

The *Arundel Castle* served the Cape route without interruption until January 1937, when she was sent to Belfast to be re-engined and lengthened, as part of the Union-Castle reconstruction programme occasioned by a speeding up of the South African mail service.

As she emerged from her 1937 refit, the *Arundel Castle* looked like a new ship ; her original four funnels were replaced by two larger, angled ones, which, along with her new raked stem, gave her a very handsome appearance. This fine "natural colour" study, a copyright photograph by Beken of Cowes, was published in the Fifties by J. Arthur Dixon Ltd., another Isle of Wight company still going strong.

The *Windsor Castle* was a victim of war in 1943 but the *Arundel Castle* continued in service until 1958. She had a 'long war' as a troopship, carrying over 200,000 men during a ten-year period and not returning to Union Castle until 1950. After a refit, she resumed Southampton-South Africa service that September, retaining her pre-war popularity until old age finally caught up with her.

On December 5th, 1958, she completed her 211th round voyage, having made 2.8 million miles of peacetime passages and another 600,000 on war service. All the ships in port and crowds of spectators gave a sad but enthusiastic send-off to the "grand old lady of the Cape fleet" when she finally left Southampton, en route to a scrapyard in Hong Kong.

It should be remembered that Union-Castle vessels also had considerable cargo capacity. On one inward voyage about 1930, the *Arundel Castle* carried cargo of over 50 different kinds, as diverse as wool, hides and skins, fruit and dairy products, mohair, ostrich feathers and Madeira wine.

CUNARD R.M.S. AQUITANIA   TONNAGE 45,650

CUNARD R.M.S. MAURETANIA   TONNAGE 31,000

The name Cunard has become synonymous with great North Atlantic liners and therefore with Southampton. The first connection is historically valid but the second needs to be qualified, because the company founded 150 years ago by Samuel Cunard was Liverpool-based for over half these years and did not transfer its principal services to Southampton until 1919 —beginning an association with the port that still continues.

Samuel Cunard (1787-1865, created a baronet in 1859) was an enterprising Canadian merchant from Halifax, Nova Scotia, who travelled to London in 1839 to secure the British mail contract for North America and enlist support to establish the British & North American Royal Mail Steam Packet Co. Ltd., becoming Cunard-White Star Ltd. after the amalgamation of 1934.

The premier Cunard operation between the wars was its prestigious express passenger service to New York, maintained by the *Mauretania, Aquitania, Berengaria* and *Queen Mary* (from 1936).

These magnificent vessels were attractively featured on publicity postcards issued by the company. These examples of the early Twenties reproduce Charles Turner's paintings, depicting the *Aquitania's* arrival at New York and the *Mauretania* speeding through the Atlantic — both splendid sights.

The *Mauretania* was one of the greatest products of the Tyneside shipyards, built by Swan Hunter, to begin her Cunard career in 1907. At nearly 32,000 tons, she and her ill-fated sister the *Lusitania* (torpedoed in 1915) were then the world's largest ships. They vied for speed records ; the *Mauretania* was very fast and seemed to grow faster with age, holding the Blue Riband for 22 years. Even after losing it to the *Bremen* in 1929, she still made voyages from New York at 27 knots.

Both as "ocean greyhound" and later as a white-hulled cruising vessel, the *Mauretania* enjoyed great esteem in shipping circles and inspired ardent admiration and affection among a far wider public.

After wartime duty as a trooper and hospital ship, she came to Southampton in June 1919 and started her first commercial voyage from her new home on March 6th, 1920. Her performance was then disappointing but she came into her own again after being refurbished and converted to oil burning by her original builders in 1921.

As the years caught up on the "Grand Old Lady", she was increasingly used for cruising ; with her white hull, she was an elegant adornment of the port scene. She also contributed to its history, as the first ship to berth at the new Western Docks, on October 19th, 1932.

Following the Cunard-White Star merger, the *Mauretania* was withdrawn from service in 1934. There was hardly a dry eye in the port when the 'Maurie' left on her final voyage to the breakers on July 1st, 1935.

ADMIRAL SIR JOHN JELLICOE ON BOARD H.M.S. 'IRON DUKE' | Reference No. 7

H. M. S. Hampshire

Southampton's naval hero of the "Great War" was Admiral Sir John Jellicoe — featured here on a card from the Photochrom Co. Ltd., one of a 1916 series reproducing pictures from the film "Britain Prepared."

John Rushworth Jellicoe was born at Southampton in 1859, of Hampshire parents whose families provided several Royal Navy Officers. His father, John Henry Jellicoe, was a captain with the Royal Mail Steam Packet Co., later its marine superintendent at Southampton, commodore of its fleet and a director of the company.

The future Admiral attended local schools and spent much of his boyhood beside, and on, Southampton Water. Entering the Royal Navy from the sail training ship Britannia in 1874, he steadily advanced in rank, then held Admiralty posts of increasing responsibility.

In 1914 he was given command of the Allied Grand Fleet. Historians still debate details of the Battle of Jutland; this 250 ship battle of 1916 was itself inconclusive, with British losses exceeding the German, but it nevertheless proved decisive in curbing effective German naval power thereafter.

Later First Sea Lord and Admiral of the Fleet, Jellicoe was created a Viscount in 1918 and an Earl in 1925. From his retirement home at Ventnor, he several times visited Southampton, most notably in 1929 to receive the honorary freedom of the Borough at a ceremony in the Empire (now Mayflower) Theatre. In 1935 he was buried in St. Paul's Cathedral, beside Nelson and Collingwood.

The original purchaser of this Stuart card (printed in Germany like so many other pre-1914 colour cards) annotated it as a memento of the 1911 Naval Review. HMS Hampshire was a 10,850 ton armoured cruiser built in 1902 — the fourth in a sequence of six ships given the county name.

Her predecessors were "wooden walls" built in 1653, 1698 and 1741 respectively. The service of the Hampshire in World War I — including involvement in the Battle of Jutland — ended suddenly on June 5th, 1916, when she sank with the loss of almost all aboard her, including Field Marshall Earl Kitchener, Secretary for War. He was headed for Russia, to consult about military operations with the Tsar's ministers and generals. Prime Minister Lloyd George had also intended going on this mission but withdrew at the last minute owing to events in Ireland. Two hours out of Scapa Flow, in rough weather, HMS Hampshire struck a mine, off Markwick Bay on the west coast of Orkney.

The name Hampshire, briefly revived in 1940 for a Free French vessel, was later bestowed on a 6,200 ton guided missile destroyer, launched from Clydebank in 1961 by Princess Margaret. The sixth HMS Hampshire ended her career prematurely when she was decommissioned in 1976; modernisation was considered uneconomic.

She made a farewell visit to Southampton in March that year, then left for her Portsmouth base, en route to the scrapyard.

"This is the *Tartar* on the day she was launched, just before she left the stocks" wrote Charlie to his girl friend in Ludlow Road − confirming the subject of this yellowing old photographic card, issued without imprint or caption.

The torpedo boat destroyer was the first of the long line of naval ships built at Woolston by the firm of John I. Thornycroft, which transferred there in 1904 to extend its operations started on the Thames at Chiswick forty years earlier. HMS *Tartar* was launched on June 25th, 1907; the *Southampton Times* reported that "the vessel, which presented a majestic appearance, glided into the Itchen in a manner which was highly gratifying to the officials in charge, giving every reason for the general congratulations which followed." Many VIPs attended the historic ceremony.

Distinguished as the first Thornycroft ship to have four funnels, the *Tartar* was a vessel of 850 tons, powered by six oil-fired boilers driving three Parsons turbines. Her contract speed was 33 knots but on her trials she developed 22,500 h.p. to register a record 35.67 knots over a measured mile off Maplin Sands. She was the first of three "Tribal" class destroyers built at Woolston, soon followed by the *Amazon* and *Nubian*. After serving on the Dover Patrol in World War I, the *Tartar* became the doyen of her class, until sold for scrap in May 1921.

J.T. Eltringham of Woolston used one of his own cards in August 1908 to send family news to a friend in Gosport. Now in Jack Foley's collection, it carries Jim's postscript "What do you think of this postcard − it is a reduction from the large photo I took." One hopes the recipient liked this fine picture of the launching of HMS *Amazon* earlier in 1908 − whether or not he commented on the "Z" being reversed in the hand-lettered caption!

The Woolston shipyard which Thornycroft took over in 1904 was originally established in 1875 by Thomas Ridley Oswald, moving down from Sunderland. In 13 years his firm (Oswald, Mordaunt & Co. from 1878) built over a hundred ships. A third were steamers (the largest was the 5,085 ton *Bitterne* of 1883) but the majority were sturdy three-masted, full-rigged, iron cargo carriers, many of which reflected the skilled hand of Hercules Linton, designer of the famous *Cutty Sark*. Some were remarkably long-lived, notably the *Wavertree* which reached its centenary in 1985, lovingly restored at South Street Seaport Museum, New York.

Oswald, Mordaunt & Co. went into liquidation in 1889 and a year later the Woolston yard was re-opened by the Southampton Naval Iron Works Ltd. This company went bankrupt in 1893 and the yard remained empty until taken in 1897 by J.G. Fay, expanding his activities from Northam. In 1900 the Woolston yard was bought by Morday, Carney & Co., who sold it to J.I. Thornycroft.

J.W. Oakley, a photographer in business at Station Road, Netley, about 1907-12, seems to have made a minor speciality of postcards featuring troopships and soldiers leaving Southampton docks. Two examples are illustrated here. The first shows artillerymen and their guns waiting embarkation from the Empress Dock; the second pictures a vessel crowded with soldiers. This was sent to his mother on November 18th, 1909 by a serviceman "just off to Jamaica" who described the ship as "very comfortable."

Such peacetime postings to garrison the old Empire were doubtless more congenial than many voyages taking troops on active service. The first major troop movements from Southampton were for the Crimean War, to which P & O steamers alone transported over 80,000 men and 20,000 horses, while the Union company had its real beginnings in chartering colliers for similar war transport purposes.

Later in the 19th century, Southampton's importance as a trooping port — with the advantage of a convenient railway connection from Aldershot — was evidenced by further extensive movements of troops and equipment for campaigns in South Africa and Egypt, as well as for duties in India. In 1894 Southampton officially replaced Portsmouth as the centre for troopship services. It remained the premier port for peacetime troop movements right up to 1962, by which time movement by sea had been superseded by air transport.

During the Boer Wars of 1899-1902, Southampton quays were kept busy with trooping activities, all accomplished smoothly and rapidly in addition to the normal business of the port. One of the highlights was an afternoon in October 1899, when five troopships were despatched in two hours, while in six days in March 1900 some 11,000 troops left Southampton aboard nine transports. Typical of the many liners involved in these Boer War movements were the *Nile* (Royal Mail), the *Assaye* (P & O) and the *Braemar Castle*. Altogether, 419 troop transports left Southampton for South Africa and the total numbers passing through the port were recorded as 25,384 officers, 502,616 men, plus 27,922 horses and large amounts of equipment and supplies.

These figures were greatly exceeded during World War I, when Southampton became Britain's No. 1 military port, under Government control, with most normal services diverted or suspended. Reorganisation of the Harbour Board early in 1914, to include representatives of government departments and wider shipping interests, had strengthened the administration of the port, enabling it to carry through with remarkable efficiency the despatch of the first expeditionary force to France in the early days of the war and a vast programme of troop and supply movements over the ensuing four years.

2025. F. G. O. Stuart.   NETLEY HOSPITAL.

H.M.H.S. "ASTURIAS" (12,002 tons).   Owners—The Royal Mail Steam Packet Company.

According to figures supplied to the Mayor by the Embarkation Commandant, in 1914-18 Southampton handled 17,186 ships (sometimes 25 sailed in a single night), conveying over 8 million personnel, nearly 860,000 horses and mules, over 15,000 guns and limbers, 180,000 vehicles and 3.5 million tons of stores, also 7.5 million parcels and mailbags.

For all too many men, Southampton was their last sight of England. Others returned as casualties; by 1920, some 2.6 million were brought back from all fronts, mostly to Southampton and Dover, which each received 1.25 million from hospital ships. Among them was the *Aquitania*, which on one journey from the Dardanelles carried nearly 5,000 men; twenty specially constructed ambulance trains ('Netley coaches') distributed them to Netley and other hospitals around the country. Even more casualties were disembarked and entrained through Southampton docks from the Somme in July 1916.

The impressive frontage of the Royal Victoria Hospital, opened in 1863, featured on many postcards; this Stuart photograph also shows the pier, then used only for exercise. Sea access influenced the choice of site but the pier was built to only half its originally proposed length of 1,200 ft., and hence not reaching deep water. In late Victorian times patients were landed there from tenders and lighters but after extension of the railway line into the hospital grounds in 1900, hospital ships berthed in the docks and casualties were conveyed direct by ambulance trains.

Over 70 military hospital ships and ambulance transports were commissioned during World War I. Besides a miscellany of smaller vessels, they included three great liners requisitioned as floating hospitals. They were the *Aquitania* (1915-17), the *Maurentania* — briefly to make three trips from the Dardanelles — and the *Britannic*.

Only completed in 1915, this 48,000 tonner never ran for the White Star Line and was sunk by a mine in the Aegean in November 1916. The *Braemer Castle* was likewise mined there but survived, afterwards serving as a base hospital at Murmansk and Archangel during the British intervention of 1918-19 against the Bolsheviks.

Another hospital ship was the Belfast-built 12,000 ton liner *Asturias*, one of the 'A' class vessels running the Royal Mail's Southampton-Buenos Aires service, from 1908 until requisitioned and converted in 1914. She is depicted on this Stuart card, a monochrome British wartime printing in different style.

Hospital ships had white hulls, with a green or red band and prominent Red Cross signs, but the Germans disregarded these markings. The *Asturias* dodged an enemy torpedo in 1915, on one of her regular cross-Channel runs (on which she often carried many more wounded than her nominal accommodation for 896) but in 1917 a 'U' boat torpedoed her off Start Point. After that attack, hospital ships ceased to be distinctively marked and were armed for self-defence. The *Asturias* was beached, then towed to Plymouth and used as an ammunition hulk. In 1919 her owners reclaimed her and rebuilt her as a cruise ship, renamed *Arcadian* in 1923. She was laid up off Southampton in 1930 and scrapped three years later in Japan.

No 12. Le S. S. Brussels coulé à l'extrémité du môle et son héroïque capitaine Fryatt, capturé par les Boches le 23 juin 1916 et fusillé le 27 juillet 1916.
The S. S. "Brussels" sunk near the extremity of Zeebrugge-mole, and her heroic Captain Fryatt, who was captured by the germans on the 23d of June 1916 and shot on the 27th of July 1916.

No 13. Le S. S. Brussels renfloué et son héroïque capitaine Fryatt, capturé par les Boches le 23 juin 1916 et fusillé à Bruges, le 27 juillet 1916.
The S. S. Brussels set afloat again and her heroic Captain Fryatt, captured by the Germans on the 23d June 1916 and shot at Bruges on the 27th. July 1916.

These two Belgian cards, from a series published about 1920 by J. Revyn of Brussels, depict the Great Eastern Railway Company's steamer *Brussels* and "her heroic Captain Fryatt, captured by the Germans on 23rd June 1916 and shot at Bruges on 27th July 1916."

Charles Algernon Fryatt, acclaimed a martyr-hero of World War I, was Southampton born in 1872, son of a seaman then living in Lower Canal Walk, afterwards in Freemantle. He spent his boyhood in the town, attending Holy Trinity and Freemantle schools, before leaving in 1883 when his father moved to Harwich to join the GER fleet. Son followed father afloat and worked his way up to become a ship's master by 1913.

From 1914, the *Brussels* was one of the GER steamers maintaining services from Harwich and Tilbury to neutral Holland. Constantly running the gauntlet of enemy attacks, Captain Fryatt became the most celebrated of the "pirate dodgers", making 143 such trips before being captured.

The publicity and Admiralty awards accorded him for the example set by his exploit of March 28th, 1915 made him a marked man in German eyes. Sighting the *U33* approaching, he ordered the *Brussels* full speed ahead straight at her, firing off rockets — giving the impression of guns — and perhaps striking a glancing blow to the submerging submarine, whose chase he escaped by making top speed into Rotterdam harbour.

On June 23rd, 1916, homeward bound from Holland, the *Brussels* was surrounded by four German destroyers and taken as a prize to Zeebrugge. Her crew spent the rest of the war as prisoners (apart from five stewardesses who were repatriated) but Captain Fryatt was court martialled at Bruges, quickly convicted of being a "franc tireur", not part of the enemy armed forces, and shot within the hour. The Germans intended his fate should deter other merchant navy captains from resisting the arrest and sinking of their ships but it proved a serious political misjudgement, arousing world-wide indignation at this "judicial murder"; Prime Minister Asquith denounced it as "this atrocious crime against the laws of nations and the usages of war."

In 1919, Captain Fryatt's body was exhumed and returned to England. It was drawn on a gun carriage to St. Paul's cathedral for a national memorial service, when, as the *Hampshire Advertiser* noted, "for the first time London saw in a state ceremonial officers and men of that great service, the merchant marine." The body was afterwards taken by special train for burial at Dovercourt, with full military honours.

After capture, the *Brussels* remained at Zeebrugge, used as a German accommodation ship, until sunk during the British raid of April 1918. She was raised in August 1919 and reconditioned. Sold by the GER in 1920, she later ran between Liverpool and Dublin as the *Lady Brussels*.

H.M.S. Southampton

ON BOARD THE ROYAL MAIL TURBINE STEAMER "VIPER".

HMS Southampton, depicted on this card from the prolific publishing house of Gale & Polden Ltd., of Aldershot and London, was the fourth of six bearers of that name.

The first was a "wooden wall" of 690 tons with 48 guns, built in 1693 by John Winter at Chapel. She became a hulk in Jamaica and was broken up in 1735 – to be followed by two further wooden 'men of war'. The third *HMS Southampton*, launched at Deptford in 1820, served as a training ship at Hull from 1867 until 1912, the year her successor was built at John Brown's Clydebank yard.

She was a 'Chatham' class light cruiser of 5,400 tons which was part of the Grand Fleet in 1914–18, gaining battle honours at Heligoland, Dogger Bank and Jutland. She particularly distinguished herself at the Battle of Jutland, when three quarters of her upper deck personnel became casualties in a fierce night action; she was badly hit and set on fire but still managed to torpedo the German cruiser *Frauenlob*. She was repaired and returned to service, until broken up in 1926.

The next *HMS Southampton* of 1936 was a 9,100 tonner, also built by Brown on the Clyde, as the name ship of a new class of cruisers. She was lost in 1941 after being attacked by German planes in the Sicilian Narrows.

The present, sixth, bearer of the city's name is a 3,800 ton guided missile destroyer, built by Vosper Thornycroft in Woolston in 1979.

"On board the Royal Mail Turbine Steamer *Viper*" is the caption of this card issued by A. Crawford of Ardrossan but used a long way from there – in April 1918 when George wrote to his sister in Ealing to say "this is the boat we are going on from Southampton; we leave tonight."

Perhaps censorship was then relaxed; certainly, George sent it through official channels – without need of a stamp, for the card was endorsed and hand stamped "On Active Service" and received a Post Office "Paid" franking.

The *Viper* was built by Fairfield for the Ardrossan–Belfast daylight service of G. & J. Burns Ltd. Of 1,713 tons, she could make 22 knots, carrying 1,700 passengers. Originally her bow was adorned with a golden viper coiling on to the bulwarks. Her service was withdrawn in 1914 and she was requisitioned by the Admiralty to carry troops across the Channel to France.

Even in 1918, there must still have been a supply of her 'on board' postcards available to them.

The *Viper* resumed her pre-war duties in 1919 but the route was given up in 1920, when she was sold to the Isle of Man Steam Packet Co. and renamed *Snaefell*. She continued in its service through World War II, until withdrawn and scrapped in 1945-6.

The chance survival of a soldier's message of 1918 provides a reminder of her war-time connection with Southampton, which might otherwise be forgotten.

The "Great War" ended on November 11th, 1918 with the signature of the Armistice – enthusiastically celebrated in Southampton until the small hours – but official "Peace" celebrations waited upon German acceptance of the Treaty of Versailles on June 28th, 1919.

National Thanksgiving services on July 6th were followed in Southampton by an extensive programme of events on Saturday, July 19th, including a great 'Mile of History' procession from the Town Quay to the Common, where an elaborate historical pageant was presented on a huge timber stage before a record crowd of some 60,000. This was followed by a fireworks display, climaxed by the lighting of a big bonfire.

The day's proceedings were inaugurated by a 21-gun salute from the old cannons on The Platform – fired for the last time. All except one went for melting down to make new weapons in 1939.

For the celebrations, the Bargate was elaborately illuminated in coloured lights, as were other corporation buildings and many business premises. Notable among them were the Union-Castle offices in Canute Road, as shown on this postcard produced by some un-named local photographer.

Union-Castle and other shipping companies had good cause to celebrate the formal end of the war in which their vessels had been heavily involved in many ways. Although the peace lasted only two decades, the inter-war years saw the heyday of great ocean liners operating world-wide services from Southampton.

Overseas trooping involved widespread shipping movements from Southampton up to and beyond World War II, mainly vessels leased from major shipping companies but including others with more distinctive histories.

On May 26th, 1920, a soldier recently arrived at Gibraltar sent home this card – "a photo of the ship I came on: thought you would like to have it." It is captioned "H.M. Transport Czar at Southampton Docks" in a style of hand lettering common to a number of shipping cards produced by a local photographer, not identified.

The *Czar,* then operated by Cunard for the British Government, retained her original name. Clyde-built in 1912 for the Danish-owned Russian American Line, this 6,500 tonner ran between Baltic and North American ports, carrying about 1,000 passengers, mostly emigrants. From 1914 she operated a New York to Archangel service but after the Russian revolution of 1917 she was taken over by the British and used as as troopship.

Returned to her owners in 1921, she resumed transatlantic service under the Baltic American Line houseflag, renamed *Estonia.* In 1930 she was transferred to Polish registry and re-styled *Pulaski*; she continued crossing the Atlantic until 1939, when she once more served the Allies as a troopship. Coming under the British flag again in 1946, as the *Empire Penryn*, she was laid up in 1948 and scrapped the following year.

SOUTHAMPTON FROM SUPERMARINE FLYING BOAT

"Southampton from Supermarine Flying Boat" is the caption to this remarkable aerial photograph taken seventy years ago and issued anonymously as a postcard. Prominent in the foreground is the World War I train ferry and pier constructed in 1917 to speed cross-Channel transport of military supplies to France, cutting the time-consuming business of man-handling cargo on and off railway wagons, barges and ships.

A special pier, 100 yards long, with a 40 yard linkspan, was built west of the Royal Pier, served by a railway extension from Southampton West (later Central) station, running behind the corporation power station and Pirelli cable works (into which there was an Army siding), down to a military marshalling yard. The service to Dieppe — the first cross-Channel train ferry — began in December 1917, using three train ferry vessels specially built on the Tyne and Clyde, each of 2,672 tons, oil-fired, with four-track decks taking 54 goods wagons.

For a second service to Cherbourg in 1918, the *Leonard*, a train ferry built at Birkenhead in 1914 for the Canadian government, was sailed across the Atlantic from Quebec (in 17 days) to become *Train Ferry No. 4*. Seen in the foreground of the postcard photograph, this was a strange-looking craft, with a framework of girders along her entire length and two very tall funnels rising above them on either side. She could operate within differences of up to 18 ft. of water, always keeping level with the quay: her three parallel tracks accommodating 39 wagons were hydraulically raised and lowered as necessary.

This service started on November 6th, 1918, only five days before the Armistice; it ended the following March, after the *Leonard* had made twelve round trips to Cherbourg. The postcard photograph must have been taken during this period. This card was used in July 1920, sent to a girl in Norfolk, Virginia, "with love from Herbert", who told her he was about to catch the evening boat to the Isle of Wight.

The first three ferry vessels and the linkspan were bought in 1922 by an Anglo-Belgian company and taken to Harwich to run a new train ferry service to Zeebrugge. The ferries came back to Southampton to help evacuate troops from Dunkirk, where No. 2 was sunk by German shellfire. Nos. 1 and 3 were later converted into landing craft, re-named *Princess Iris* and *Princess Daffodil*. The latter was sunk by a mine when carrying locomotives from Southampton to Cherbourg in March 1945 but No. 1 survived: reconstructed in 1946, it served as the *Essex Ferry* until 1957.

Meanwhile, the Canadian vessel *Leonard* had been acquired by the Anglo-Saxon Petroleum Company and converted into an oil carrier, re-named *Limax*, which lasted until 1932.

The specially built pier at Southampton, disused from 1922, remained until 1929, when it was dismantled and removed at the start of reclamation work for the new Western Docks and the creation of Mayflower Park.

The Royal Pier, SOUTHAMPTON.

1676. 3

The lower card is a pedestrian's view of the Royal Pier; close neighbour of the temporary linkspan, it survives today — but only just.

SOUTHAMPTON. HIGH STREET TOWN QUAY FROM AN AEROPLANE. (4320)

1203 C. R. Hoffmann AERIAL VIEW OF SOUTHAMPTON DOCKS, SHOWING NINE OF THE WORLD'S LARGEST LINERS.
Southampton. GROSS TONNAGE 316,000 TONS.

This aerial view of the High Street and Town Quay in the early Twenties comes from a set of six cards published by the Photochrom Co. of Tunbridge Wells. Dominating the waterside scene in the left foreground is the impressive Victorian building, styled 'H' warehouse by the Harbour Board but long known as Geddes warehouse after the Board's surveyor, Donald Geddes, whose name appears with that of the builder, H. W. Bull, on the 1866 tablet high on the west gable wall.

The site was earlier occupied by the Customs Commissioners but in 1847 they moved to a new Customs House (later Union-Castle House) in Canute Road and the Corporation transferred the lease to the Harbour Board. It erected a two-storey baggage warehouse there in 1851, flanking the Corn Exchange, a lofty Italianate building, now Seaway House.

In the 1860s three storeys were added and the resulting five-storey block was extended to the west on a six-storey plan. Geddes nicely combined everything in the frontage, barely identifiable as the produce of separate phases of building.

It outlived its purpose after the post-war decline in passenger liner traffic and was bought back by the Corporation, which in 1983 leased it to a developer for conversion into luxury flats and an up-market restaurant.

"Aerial view of Southampton Docks, showing nine of the world's largest liners, gross tonnage 316,000 tons" is the caption to one of the most popular Hoffmann cards (1203). Also reproduced as a postcard in W.H. Smith's "Kingsway" series (S.19429), it and similar views nostalgically document the palmiest days of the great ocean liners associated with Southampton between the Wars.

On the Hoffmann card, their names and individual tonnages are neatly lettered. From left to right, they are the *Empress of Australia*, *Aquitania*, *Majestic*, *Mauretania*, *Berengaria*, *Homeric*, *Arandora Star*, *Alcantara* and *Empress of Britain* — a miniature picture gallery of the best-loved 'greats'.

The *Empress of Britain* made her maiden voyage from Southampton on May 27th, 1931 and the *Homeric* ended her Atlantic service in 1932. In 1931 the *Aquitania* arrived on November 3rd and sailed on the 5th, so this photograph was almost certainly taken between those dates.

The wide range of shipping cards published in his father's name by O.W. Hoffmann found ready buyers in the busy docks, not only among passengers arriving and departing, with friends and relatives coming to welcome them or see them off, but also the hosts of day-trippers brought by train and coach excursions. In the mid-Thirties, O.W. Hoffmann had 18-20 girls serving in six shops and kiosks in the Old and New Docks, supplemented by six boys who set up portable stands at strategic points, where they offered "Today's Ship Photographs" at 2d. each or 7 for a shilling. On a good day, Hoffmann postcard sales exceeded 10,000.

R.M.S.
"ATLANTIS."

PASSING COWES on the way from Cherbourg to Southampton.

Kenneth Shoesmith was one of those artists who became synonymous with the style of an age because he helped to create it.

In 1909 the Yorkshireman joined the Royal Mail fleet as a junior officer. Two years later he showed his talent by winning a prize in a staff competition for publicity material. He continued afloat, serving in several vessels out of Southampton and rising to the rank of First Officer, before deciding to take up commercial art full-time.

Shoesmith worked for various different shipping companies, including Cunard and Canadian Pacific, and was involved in producing posters, magazines, menu cards and other forms of publicity, as well as postcards. It is for his work with Royal Mail that he is now best remembered — as he himself would doubtless have wished, for at his request his ashes were scattered from the stern of the Royal Mail liner *Asturias* in 1939.

Shoesmith's paintings of Royal Mail liners in many different locations were used by the company for colourful postcards, such as these, distributed widely between the wars to promote its regular services as "The Comfort Route" and publicise its pleasure cruises, which took in Norway and Iceland as well as the West Indies, Mediterranean and "Round Britain".

Of all the Royal Mail ships painted by Shoesmith, the *Atlantis* was his most frequent subject, depicted in many of the exotic places which she visited as a cruise liner.

Built in 1913 as the *Andes,* she began her Southampton connection on the River Plate route. After eventful war service, she returned to this duty in 1919, continuing until 1929, when she was converted into a white-painted cruise ship renamed *Atlantis.*

Shoesmith helped to create the popular holiday image of this vessel, which she maintained for ten years. After the outbreak of World War II, she was converted at Southampton to become Hospital Ship No. 33, equipped to carry some 600 patients, with a medical staff of 100. In this role, her varied duties extended from evacuating casualties from Norway in 1940 to taking wounded American soldiers from Europe to New York in 1945. Between 1948 and 1952 she was chartered to carry British immigrants to Australia, before withdrawal for scrapping ended her existence after 39 years.

Some Shoesmith compositions were generalised, rather than specific ship pictures, like this colourful evocation of a liner "passing Cowes on the way from Cherbourg to Southampton." She could have been either the *Asturias* or the *Alcantara,* both familiar sights in local waters for thirty years until withdrawn in the late Fifties.

Many shipping companies commissioned artists to produce publicity material, of which postcards were an important aspect. Besides depicting the liners, it was their function to help promote them to potential passengers by giving attractive impressions of their grandeur, style and atmosphere. The artists responsible for these two cards, showing the last vessels actually built for the White Star Line, certainly did a good job for their clients.

Cards like this, featuring an actual white star, were produced for most White Star liners, for use aboard and distribution through hotels and shipping agents. The name and address of the White Star Line Agency at Llanelli is printed on the back of this reproduction of William McDowell's fine painting, along with text proclaiming "M.V. *Britannic*, 27,000 tons, Britain's Largest Motor Vessel; length 680 feet, breadth 82 feet."

Built by Harland & Wolff at Belfast, the *Britannic* (the third White Star ship of that name) began service in 1930 between Liverpool and New York. Five years later, after the Cunard-White Star merger, she was transferred to the London-Le Havre-Southampton route. Her two squat funnels gave her a distinctive profile, although the forward one was a dummy, which housed her radio equipment.

Taken over as a troopship, she carried some 180,000 troops during the war. After refitting, she resumed Liverpool-New York sailings in 1948. In later years, as a cruise liner, she often called at Southampton, until withdrawn in 1960 — the last vessel to retain White Star colours.

James Mann's painting of the *Georgic,* used for a Cunard-White Star publicity card of the mid-Thirties, presents an unusual and dramatic picture of what was once the world's largest motor ship, with large areas of flat monochrome surrounds serving to highlight her bulky, squat appearance.

Delivered from her Belfast builders in 1932, the 27,759 ton *Georgic* had a pre-war career similar to that of her sister ship but her wartime experiences were eventfully different. Likewise doing duty as a trooper, she was bombed and set on fire at Suez in July 1914. Beached, salvaged and temporarily patched up, she was towed to Bombay for repairs to enable her to limp half way round the world back to Belfast. There she was rebuilt as an improved model troopship, esteemed by servicemen as the 'Super Trooper'. Alterations included removal of her forward funnel and mast.

Acquired by the Ministry of Transport and used for trooping from 1944, she also carried emigrants from Britain to Australia in 1949 (under P&O charter). In the early 1950s she was chartered back by Cunard for summer voyages between Southampton and New York, on a one-class tourist basis, and to bring immigrants from the West Indies to Britain. The *Georgic* was finally withdrawn in 1955 for scrapping.

SOUVENIR OF THE VISIT OF H.R.H. PRINCE OF WALES TO SOUTHAMPTON JUNE 27TH 1924.

COPYRIGHT F. T. LEWIS. SOUTHAMPTON HARBOUR BOARD OFFICES AND "MAJESTIC" IN FLOATING DOCK.

This "Souvenir of the visit of H.R.H. Prince of Wales to Southampton, June 27th, 1924" must have been rushed out by some local photographer; he did not put his name on his postcards.

The Prince, later Edward VIII, Duke of Windsor, came to inaugurate the world's largest floating dry dock. This had become an urgent necessity to accommodate the largest Atlantic liners using the port in the early Twenties. Manoeuvring them into the Trafalgar Dock with only inches to spare had often involved rare skills of navigation.

The Southern Railway (which had incorporated the LSWR under the 1923 railway grouping scheme) ordered a huge new floating dock, capable of receiving and lifting − within four hours − vessels of 60,000 tons. A site for it was dredged between the Town Quay and Berth 50. Built on Tyneside by Armstrong Whitworth & Co. and towed to Southampton, this much admired 20,000 ton work of engineering was 960 ft. long and 134 ft. wide, with side walls of 70 ft. Its internal floor area was about 3½ acres.

The Prince of Wales, then very popular, was enthusiastically acclaimed all along the bedecked route of his open car tour, which took in a lot more than the floating dock. From the West Station he was driven across the floating bridge to visit the Supermarine works, then back to inspect the new engineering marvel and operate the levers to submerge it. After lunch aboard the *Aquitania*, he boarded the paddler *Duchess of Fife*, which duly snapped the ribbon across the floating dock entrance. Afternoon visits included the Cenotaph, University College and RSH Hospital, ending with tea in the Royal Pier pavilion.

The floating dry dock met requirements for overhaul and repair of major ocean liners for barely a decade. It was superseded by the King George V Graving Dock, No. 7 Dry Dock, opened in 1933. Although not regularly in use thereafter, it remained in position until February 1940, when it was taken to Portsmouth for Admiralty purposes. Surplus there in 1959, it was sold for use at Rotterdam, by a company which ceased business in 1983. The dock was then acquired by new owners from Brazil but it never reached there, being wrecked off the Spanish coast while under tow.

In 1924-33 the sight of an ocean giant like the *Berengaria* or *Majestic* elevated completely above the water in the floating dock never ceased to impress beholders. It provided a photogenic subject for many postcards, particularly when the liner appeared alongside the Harbour Board's new offices, as in this F.T. Lewis card of the *Majestic* − still being sold and used in 1935, when the scene was only a vivid memory.

The Harbour Board building, officially opened on September 8th, 1925 by Admiral of the Fleet the Earl Jellicoe of Scapa (page 52), was much admired. It was designed by Edward Cooper Poole, who followed his father as the Board's surveyor and engineer and served it for 48 years until his death in 1935 − a few weeks before he would have retired at 70.

E. Cooper Poole was also the architect for reconstructing the approach and entrance to the Royal Pier in 1926-27. Shown here on a postcard from R.F. Fielder, a little known small publisher, this whimsically attractive composition replaced the more mundane buildings for which he had also been responsible in 1890-92.

Southampton was a port, not a seaside resort, and its pier was primarily functional, not recreational, in origin and purpose. It was nevertheless very popular as a promenading place, affording fine views of great liners and the general shipping scene, along with the benefits of sea air, inhaled without the need to risk seasickness or incur the expense of boarding a steamer!

The Pier Pavilion was long the venue for concerts, dances and other entertainments. Although it and the pier itself are now dilapidated and disused, the main approach buildings enjoy a new lease of life as a licensed restaurant.

In the 1920s, since the new Harbour Board offices were given a prominent clock tower, it was not thought necessary to have another at the nearby pier, so the old clock was dismantled and stored. Later, at the request of (Sir) Sidney Kimber, the Harbour Board gave it to the Corporation, to be incorporated into the pavilion of the new municipal golf course, opened in 1935.

The Southern Railway managers had a keen eye to public relations and publicity. Besides promoting the docks in their own right and as a source of increased passenger and goods traffic, they attracted many extra railway customers as day visitors. Excursion trains, coaches and steamers regularly brought thousands of ordinary folk to view the busy docks scene, admire the floating dock and accept the invitation to "look over a luxury liner in Southampton docks."

Those who came on "inspection days" may never have had the prospect of travelling on one but it was all good business; during the Thirties sightseers visiting the docks numbered some half million a year. For them, the Southern Railway produced "A Souvenir of Southampton Docks", an attractive illustrated booklet — "a day's pleasure in potted form, to show your friends, before they too visit the Docks."

Private souvenir postcards also found a ready sale among the groups which happily posed beside a board identifying the occasion. "Viewing RMS *Aquitania* and Southern Railway's Floating Dry Dock, Southampton" were the families featured on this card, which is annotated on the back "taken at Southampton Docks which we visited August 8th, 1929." Visitors were greatly impressed by the scale of what they saw. The card of the *Majestic* illustrated on the next page was sent by a lady to her son in Lewes, telling him "we have been over this today — 1,100 crew, 3,000 passengers, about half the population of Lewes when she is fully booked up. It is like a floating Metropole, only larger."

1001 C. R. HOFFMANN.   R.M.S. "MAJESTIC" 56,551 Tons
The Largest Ship in the World. Length 956 Ft Breadth 100 Ft

1207 C. R. Hoffmann,   White Star Line. R.M.S. "MAJESTIC."   56,551 Tons.
Southampton   The Largest Steamer in the World.
1st CLASS LOUNGE ENTRANCE.

An appropriate choice in 1924 to inaugurate the C.R. Hoffmann series of shipping cards (whose numbering began at 1001) was the White Star liner *Majestic*. Proudly proclaimed "the largest ship in the world", at 56,551 tons, with a length of 956 ft. and a beam of 100 ft., she was the company's fastest liner, maintaining service speeds of 24-25 knots.

She started her maiden Southampton-New York voyage on May 20th, 1922, nearly eight years after her launching — at the famour Blohm & Voss yard in Hamburg, intended for the Hamburg American Line under the name *Bismarck*. By the Treaty of Versailles reparations arrangements, the half-finished ship was transferred to Britain, along with the *Imperator* (*Berengaria*), the latter going to Cunard, the former to White Star, to be renamed *Majestic*.

From 1920, she was altered and refitted at Hamburg, under the supervision of Harland & Wolff. Her departure down the Elbe in March 1922 was watched resentfully by silent or weeping crowds; at her handover, the White Star crew boarded over the starboard side as the Germans clambered over the port side. The change of ownership as a bloodless prize of war was highlighted in August 1922 when King George V and Queen Mary visited the liner in Cowes Roads. At the King's request, the Royal Standard, brought over from the royal yacht, was hoisted at the *Majestic*'s mainmast as Their Majesties stepped aboard her.

The King and Queen made a long and extensive tour of the *Majestic*, finding much to interest them — not surprisingly, for she truly lived up to her name. The six-deck vessel was magnificently appointed on the grand scale, primarily for 750 first class passengers, who enjoyed a style of ornate luxury that can only be marvelled at today. A glimpse of it is given by this later Hoffmann card (1207) depicting the entrance to the first class lounge.

The floating mansion boasted among its lavish accommodation a 678 seat restaurant, the tallest ever fitted into a ship; an elegant "Palm Court" tree-lined avenue and a swimming pool pillared in classic splendour. Besides the VIPs and millionaires travelling first, the Majestic also carried 545 second and 850 third class passengers, with 1,000 crew (to whom she was affectionately known as the "Magic Stick").

Her size made it very difficult to manoeuvre her into the Trafalgar dry dock, hence the provision of the larger floating dry dock in 1924. Ten years later, she was the first ship to enter the King George V Graving Drock, on January 19th, 1934.

Between 1922 and 1936, the *Majestic* made over 200 North Atlantic return trips, covering 1.25 million miles. Two years after the Cunard-White Star merger of 1934, she was withdrawn from service, to be converted by Thornycrofts into a naval training ship for 2,000 boys at Rosyth, HMS *Caledonia*. Her end came in 1939, when she caught fire while being refitted for wartime transport work.

Besides the coloured publicity cards reproducing paintings of its great liners (page 51), the Cunard Line also promoted them by distributing other cards giving artists' impressions of their extensive accommodation and internal arrangements, such as these two of the *Aquitania*, issued in the early Twenties.

Launched at John Brown's yard on Clydebank in 1913, the 45,600 tonner was the last of the great passenger liners completed before World War I. She had a long working life of 36 years — much of it associated with Southampton, from the time of her arrival at the port in June 1919, to make the first advertised Cunard voyage to New York, right through to her final departure to be scrapped in 1950. The *Aquitania* is still affectionately remembered by many Southampton folk and generations of shiplovers as the last — and in many cases, the only — 'four-stacker' they ever saw.

R.M.S. Aquitania
(SECTIONAL VIEW)

Built to partner the *Mauretania* and *Lusitania* on the North Atlantic service, she made a few Liverpool-New York voyages in the summer of 1914 but in August was taken over as an armed merchant cruiser. A collision cut short these duties and she became a hospital ship (page 55), then carried American troops to Europe in 1918.

After conversion from coal to oil burning in 1920 (which cut her stokehold hands from 350 to 50) she ran Southampton-New York services until 1939 — at over 24 knots after being fitted with new propellers in 1936.

The *Aquitania* was built to carry some 600 first class passengers, another 600 in second class and over 2,000 in third class and steerage, with a crew of nearly 1,000. Emigrants from Britain, Ireland and many European countries had provided the mainstay of expanding liner services across the Atlantic up to 1914 but American legislation of 1917-24 drastically reduced, then virtually ended, the flow of immigrants into the United States.

While still catering primarily for the rich and famous, Cunard and other transatlantic lines offset this loss of traffic by cultivating new categories of travellers — the 'old home traffice' of immigrants who had done well enough to be able to visit their homelands and a developing mass market in American tourists of comparatively modest means, particularly teachers and students.

For their benefit, steerage accommodation was revamped as Tourist or Third class. This Cunard postcard publicised the *Aquitania*'s facilities, with pictures of smoking room, dining room, covered promenade deck and "4 berth room."

The card at the left offers a 'sectional view', neatly illustrating the hierarchy of the liner's eight decks, from first class state rooms, lounges and restaurant down to the third class dining saloon at the water line.

1160. C. R. Hoffmann.
Southampton.

R.M.S. "AQUITANIA."
Carolean Smoking Room.

46,600 Tons

R.M.S. "AQUITANIA"

For well-to-do Americans during the Prohibition era of 1920-33, Cunard liners offered the additional attraction of plentiful supplies of liquor, especially quality whisky and brandy, at a fraction of the cost of inferior bootlegged spirits back home. Aboard the *Aquitania*, the elegant surroundings of the "Carolean Smoking Room" (pictured here on a Hoffmann card of the late Twenties) must have witnessed a lot of drinking as well as cigar-smoking — all under the benevolent gaze of the 'Merrie Monarch', Charles II, whose portrait hung above the imitation fireplace.

It is said that some well-heeled passengers could not resist the temptation to over-indulge, even to the extent of having to be carried ashore on stretchers to the boat trains awaiting them in Southampton!

The Carolean Smoking Room, Palladian Lounge and other public rooms on the *Aquitania* were designed by Arthur Davis, the London partner of Charles Mewès — the French architect responsible for the elaborate décor of several pre-1914 HAPAG liners. The ornate interior of the *Aquitania* represented the high point of 'Edwardian' ship architecture, in line with Cunard policy of giving passengers on its 'floating palace' the illusion of still being in a hotel ashore.

The *Aquitania* ran Southampton-New York services in partnership with the *Mauretania* and *Berengaria*, then from 1936 with the *Queen Mary*. Altogether, the long-serving Cunarder carried 1.2 million passengers over three million miles on 443 commercial voyages. Her withdrawal was planned for 1940, when the *Queen Elizabeth* was scheduled to take over, but the outbreak of war added another decade to her working life.

In 1938 she made a one-off trip as a trooper taking reinforcements to the British garrison in Egypt. In 1939 she resumed the role of troopship, which lasted until 1948. The *Aquitania* did not return to commercial service but between May 1948 and November 1949 made a dozen 'austerity' round voyages betwen Southampton and Halifax, carrying emigrants and other sponsored passengers.

Even in 1948, life aboard her seemed good. This card was sent with the message "Mid-Atlantic, 12.9.48. Having a lovely rest in spite of the weather which is not very nice. Plenty of food & still able to enjoy it! Still can't believe I'm on my way to S. I'll wake up someday soon I expect. Got through Customs OK but whether I will the other end remains to be seen."

Affectionately known as "the ship beautiful" and "Old Irrepressible", the *Aquitania* finally went to the breakers in 1950 — after her furniture and fittings had been auctioned off in Southampton docks.

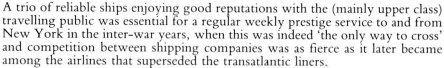

1028. C. R. Hoffmann Southampton.　　　R.M.S. "BERENGARIA."　　52.226 TONS
Length 919 ft.　　　Breadth 98 ft.

1199 C. R. Hoffmann Southampton.　　　R.M.S. "BERENGARIA."　　52.226 Tons
BALLROOM.

A trio of reliable ships enjoying good reputations with the (mainly upper class) travelling public was essential for a regular weekly prestige service to and from New York in the inter-war years, when this was indeed 'the only way to cross' and competition between shipping companies was as fierce as it later became among the airlines that superseded the transatlantic liners.

Completing Cunard's threesome in the Twenties was the *Berengaria*, now less remembered than her consorts but in her day an equally prestigious liner, which served Cunard long and well until 1938. Continuing the Cunard liking for "ia" endings, she was named after the consort of Richard the Lion Heart – whereas most other Cunarders of her era were given the names of imperial provinces of ancient Rome.

Shown here on a popular Hoffmann card, first issued in 1924, the *Berengaria* began life as the HAPAG liner *Imperator*, built at Hamburg in 1913. At 52,226 tons, she was then the world's largest, designed to impress by her size, opulence and comfort. On her maiden voyage in June 1913 she received a civic welcome when first calling at Southampton. On her fourth voyage, she arrived in New York with over 5,000 people aboard, the most that ever crossed.

Having spent the war years in port at Hamburg, she was taken over by the Allies and acquired in 1920 by Cunard, renamed and converted to oil fuel, with her passenger capacity reduced to a more manageable total of 2,700, served by 1,050 crew.

In the decade up to 1914, Albert Ballin, the leading spirit of the HAPAG company, entrusted the French architect Charles Mewès with the layout and decoration of the public rooms aboard its new liners, intended to be the world's biggest and best. Mewès had made his name in association with César Ritz, establishing a chain of super-luxury hotels. No effort and little expense were spared in creating palatially spacious first class facilities, elegantly adorned in 18th century French styles.

Mewès was not responsible for the huge bronze eagle initially fitted to the bow of the *Imperator*; this symbol of German imperial might soon suffered storm damage and was removed.

Perhaps the grandest feature of the German liner was the Ritz-Carlton à la carte restaurant and winter garden, which the *Berengaria* refit turned into a ballroom and palm court, suggesting a Monte Carlo patio – as shown on this Hoffmann card of 1930 vintage. The original Pompeian swimming pool, which Mewès based on the one he had designed for the RAC Club in Pall Mall, was left little changed. Cunard had the heavy marble baths in first class cabins replaced with cast iron – with an eye to improving stability, for the *Imperator* had been notoriously top-heavy and liable to list. Cunard did not change all the fittings; taps were left marked *auf* and *zu* and ash-trays remained lettered *Zigarren* – but all '13' doors were renumbered!

Most of the original Gallic décor survived to serve for 25 years on the *Berengaria*, which one Cunard captain called "a gleaming and bejewelled ferryboat for the rich and titled."

1026 C. R. HOFFMANN.   UNITED STATES LINES, S.S. "LEVIATHAN."
The World's Greatest Liner, 59,956 Tons.   Length 950 Ft.   Breadth 100 Ft. 6 Ins.

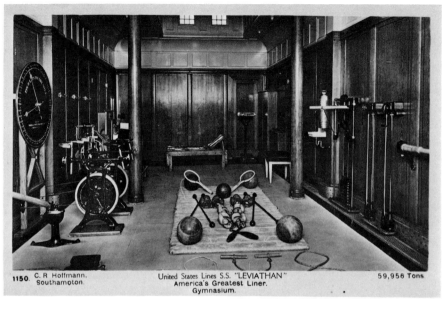

1150   C. R. Hoffmann.   United States Lines S.S. "LEVIATHAN"   59,956 Tons
Southamoton.   America's Greatest Liner.
Gymnasium.

"The World's Greatest Liner, 59,956 tons" was the claim of the United States Lines, adopted for the caption of this 1924 Hoffman postcard picture of the *Leviathan* but her nominal tonnage was boosted as a promotional ploy, secured by an unusual method of calculation. Later printings and other Hoffmann cards styled her "America's Greatest Liner", which was true enough, even after her tonnage was more conventionally re-assessed in 1932 as 48,943.

The *Leviathan* was originally the German liner *Vaterland*, 54,282 tons, the last of the HAPAG pre-war giants, built at Hamburg by Blohm & Voss. She made her maiden voyage, calling at Southampton, in May 1914. The outbreak of war caught her in New York, where she remained. In 1917 she was taken over as an American war prize and, like the *Imperator* and others of "the American Fleet the Kaiser built us", converted into a troophip, carrying over 10,000 'doughboys' at a time to France. They soon dubbed her the 'Levi Nathan' — her new name was believed to have been suggested by President Wilson himself.

The Americans retained her as reparations and after an extensive refit (directed by William Gibbs, later to design the *United States* — see page 93) and conversion to oil, she resumed commercial service to Southampton in July 1923. The *Leviathan* could carry 3,200 passengers but rarely sailed more than half full. She became an expensive "white elephant", vulnerable to the depression of 1929: she spent most of the Thirties laid up, until making a final crossing to the breakers at Rosyth in 1938.

The *Leviathan* retained much of the elegance given to the *Vaterland* by Charles Mewès (at his desire, her funnel uptakes were divided up the sides of the vessel to allow long central vistas down the length of the decks) but luxury accommodation alone could not attract enough first class passengers to make her pay, while curtailment of immigration into the United States severely reduced basic third class traffic. The *Leviathan* lacked a comparable running mate to operate regular services but, more decisively, she was perforce a 'dry ship' throughout the Prohibition era.

Rich Americans who enjoyed drinking obviously chose to travel under any flag other than that of the United States. The crew of the *Leviathan* had no choice but when the liner docked at Southampton, many of them seized the opportunity to make up for their long 'dry' days aboard. Stories are still told of how local publicans braced themselves for these thirsty invaders!

Aboard the liner there were, of course, various diversions and entertainments to help passengers keep their minds off alcohol. Consuming large amounts of rich food was a tradition on the great liners, doubtless followed on the *Leviathan* (unless the North Atlantic was unkind), even though there were no choice wines to accompany meals or spirits to follow. One wonders, however, how many passengers actually sought to maintain fitness by work-outs in the liner's gymnasium — here pictured on a Hoffmann card of the late Twenties; perhaps some found the prospect too daunting!

Tudor House Gardens, Southampton

THE KING GEORGE V GRAVING DOCK—SOUTHAMPTON DOCKS.
THE DOCK NEARING COMPLETION.

Photo by Evening Standard

Issued anonymously in the late Twenties, this postcard photograph of the garden of Tudor House (from 1912 the Borough's first museum) spans the centuries. Beyond the rebuilt archway from the medieval priory of St. Denys and the shell of the Norman merchant's house, incorporated into the town wall along the shore in the aftermath of the French raid of 1338, can be seen the cranes and dredgers engaged in changing the local topography to create the new Western Docks.

In the inter-war years, concentration on passenger rather than cargo traffic cushioned Southampton against trade depression and the creation of a larger railway organisation provided the resources to extend the docks to meet increased demand for long deep-water berths. By 1911 the area of the Eastern Docks had been fully exploited and the LSWR had considered siting additional facilities in the Woolston-Netley area but Southern Railway planners preferred to develop new linear quays along the Test from the Royal Pier to Millbrook Point.

The ambitious £10 million scheme conceived by Sir Herbert Walker involved the largest land reclamation scheme then undertaken in Britain (400 acres) and vast concrete and filling works to provide some 8,000 ft. of straight quays, with related transit sheds, reception buildings and railway lines, flanked by a large area for development as an industrial estate. Work began in January 1927 and was completed in 1934, although berths were brought into use from October 1932.

At the far end of the "Extension Quay" – as the new docks were initially called – contractors took over the site on June 30th, 1931 to begin work on "No. 7 Dry Dock", the largest of its kind, 1,200 ft. long and 135 ft. wide, designed to take liners of up to 100,000 tons.

Thousands of men laboured day and night to excavate about 2 million tons of earth and lay some 750,000 tons of concrete. Their progress in constructing what was to be styled the "King George V Graving Dock" was publicised by Southern Railway postcards. "Aerial view shewing the completed dock before fitting of gate and dredging of entrance" was the title on the back of this one, which did not miss the chance of proclaiming "Southampton Docks owned and managed by the Southern Railway."

The official opening by King George V on July 26th, 1933 was the occasion for great celebrations, beginning with massed bands and choirs entertaining spectators for two hours before the Royal Yacht *Victoria & Albert* arrived to break a ribbon across the entrance. After the King had declared the dock open, Queen Mary received from the SR chairman "a cup containing Empire wine, with which she christened the dock". It was not actually used by a liner until January 1934, when the *Majestic* entered it for overhaul.

The new docks highlighted expanding port activity. By 1938, over 18.6 million tons of shipping passed through Southampton, compared with 11.4 million in 1928, and it ranked third overall after London and Liverpool, which handled much greater cargo traffic.

7104. THE "EMPRESS OF BRITAIN" & "EMPRESS OF AUSTRALIA"
BERTHED AT SOUTHAMPTON.

1213 C. R. Hoffmann,
Southampton   "EMPRESS OF AUSTRALIA."
PRINCE OF WALES SUITE.

Opposite South Western House in Canute Road is a little used railway entrance to the Eastern Docks, beside which can still be discerned the painted lettering of the pre-war advertising slogan "Canadian Pacific Spans the World".

This curious survival harks back to the Twenties and Thirties, when the boast was literally true − you could travel from Southampton to the Far East, via the Atlantic, Canada overland and the Pacific, on the "All Empire Route" of the company which proclaimed itself "the world's greatest transportation system" which "bridged two oceans and linked four continents."

Following completion of the 3,000 mile railway between Montreal and Vancouver in 1887, the Canadian Pacific Railway company steadily extended its steamship services, entering the North Atlantic trade in 1903. Originally running to Liverpool, its liners first called at Southampton in 1919 and established a regular service to Quebec in 1922.

Southampton soon became familiar with the "Empresses" (as many CP ships were named), with their buff funnels and black hulls or all white hulls and upperworks.

For this card − one of a series issued without a publisher's imprint − two of the best-known were photographed in the 1930s berthed at the Western Docks, with 101 shed on the right. The *Empress of Australia* is prominent in the foreground, with the *Empress of Britain* beyond her at the left. They were probably between cruises, on which both were then frequently employed.

The *Empress of Australia* was originally built at Stettin, as the *Tirpitz* for the Hamburg American Line, but was taken as part of German war reparations and allocated to Canadian Pacific.

She first operated on its Pacific services out of Vancouver (on one, she was caught in port at Yokohama during the devastating earthquake of 1923) but in 1927 she was brought back to make Atlantic crossings from Southampton. On her second voyage, her passengers included the Prince of Wales and Prime Minister Stanley Baldwin, going to Canada for the celebrations of its 60 years of Confederation. Another Royal occasion was in 1939, when the *Empress of Australia* took the King and Queen to begin their memorable tour of the Dominion; they returned aboard the *Empress of Britain*.

At 21,833 gross tons, the *Empress of Australia* was not one of the larger vessels crossing the North Atlantic but its wealthy passengers still travelled in a style of luxury matching that of her bigger rivals. This Hoffmann card showing her elegant and fashionably named Prince of Wales Suite probably derived from a company publicity photograph, about 1933.

The *Empress of Australia* underwent a dramatic change of use in 1939, when she became a troopship. She continued in this role until scrapped in 1952.

13233. SOUTHAMPTON, EMPRESS OF BRITAIN—JUDGE/ES

1190 C. R. Hoffmann, Southampton.   Canadian Pacific Liner. "EMPRESS OF BRITAIN." KNICKERBOCKER BAR.   42.500 Tons.

The *Empress of Britain*, at 42,348 tons the largest Canadian Pacific liner, was a handsome ship, which had an existence of only nine years. She was launched from John Brown's yard on June 11th, 1930 by the Prince of Wales, who also came to see her off on her maiden voyage from Southampton to Canada on May 27th, 1931.

Hailed as "The Pride of the Clyde", she was rated one of the outstanding ships of her age. Her innovations included the first ship-to-shore radio telephone system, as well as the largest swimming pool in any vessel then afloat and a large ballroom, with a domed ceiling depicting the night sky at the time of her launching. A crew of 700 served her 1,095 passengers. She was a fast ship, initially outpaced only by the *Bremen* and *Europa*.

During the summer months she operated on the St. Lawrence route, undoubtedly the most prestigious vessel ever to grace it. She must have made a fine sight going up that river or Southampton Water, with three massive funnels (68 ft. high and 35 ft. in diameter, proudly illuminated at night) atop her white upperworks and hull, which carried a blue line and a green waterline.

After 100 Canadian voyages from Southampton and 16 cruises, mainly from New York, the *Empress of Britain* became a troopship. In October 1940, homeward bound from Egypt, she was set ablaze by a German bomber off Ireland and later torpedoed while under tow.

Canadian Pacific revived her name in 1957 but never returned to Southampton after the war to operate a regular passenger service.

In his speech at the launching of the *Empress of Britain*, the Prince of Wales said "This vessel may be considered in construction as the last word in shipbuilding, and as regards her appointments she will have no rivals . . . I note that, in addition to her squash racquets court, gymnasium and swimming bath, fortunate passengers in this ship have at their disposal an open air tennis court, Turkish and electric baths, a dental surgery, ultra voilet ray department and even a beauty parlour. The ballroom will be decorated by Sir John Lavery, Mr Dulac is being given a free hand in the smoking room and Mr Frank Brangwyn in the dining room, while those who frequent the cocktail bar can let their imagination run riot in a rosy haze amid the fantastic humour of Mr Heath Robinson."

Representative of the "appointments" that so impressed the Prince was the Knickerbocker Bar, subject of another Hoffmann card of the early Thirties.

Intended from the outset to serve for cruising in the winter season, the *Empress of Britain* soon acquired a reputation as a leader in her field. She was designed with an eye to passing through the Panama Canal and visiting as many ports as possible.

Her luxurious comforts were not cheap, of course. Even in the Thirties, prices for her 128-day, 30,000 mile cruises from New York ranged from $2,150 up to $16,150 — with servants carried for $1,750 a head!

901-19. 'WARWICK CASTLE,' IN DOCKS, SOUTHAMPTON.

S.S. "ARANDORA STAR" AT BALHOLM.   BLUE STAR LINE CRUISE.

Photographed for this anonymous card at Berth 39 (now Queen Elizabeth Passenger Terminal) is the 20,445 ton *Warwick Castle*. She was the last of a quintet of new passenger motor ships built by Harland & Wolff at Belfast between 1926 and 1931 for the Union-Castle Line. The company liked motor ships more than most other lines and kept building them up to 1948.

The other vessels of the twin funnelled series typical of the breed (also Royal Mail and White Star liners) were the *Winchester Castle*, *Carnarvon Castle*, *Llangibby Castle* and *Dunbar Castle*. The *Warwick Castle* was not a frequent caller at Southampton as she mainly operated on the Round Africa service, from London. She had a short life of only 11 years before becoming the victim of a 'U' boat.

Just astern of her in the picture can be seen a prominent feature of the pre-war dock scene, the International Cold Store at Berth 40. Further astern at Berth 41 is probably an Orient liner, while a four-funnelled Cunarder lies at the Ocean Dock.

The massive Cold Store (capacity 1.7 million cubic feet) handled refrigerated cargoes of all kinds, direct from the ships for distribution, mainly by rail. Much of its contents was butter and margarine, which fed a dramatic fire lasting several weeks after the store was set alight by German bombs in August 1940.

The Blue Star Line was one of Britain's larger shipping companies; most of its interests were in refrigerated cargoes but it also ran luxury passenger services between Liverpool and South America. Only its *Arandora Star*, operating full-time as an up-market cruise liner, was a regular caller at Southampton in the Thirties.

She was built by Cammell Laird at Birkenhead in 1927, as part of a five-ship fleet for South American service but the 1929 Depression obliged the company to change its plans. Originally named *Arandora* (*Star* was added in 1929 to end confusion with Royal Mail ships having similar names), this steam turbine liner was rebuilt and refitted for cruising, with her tonnage increased from 12,847 to 14,694 and her capacity raised from 164 to 354 passengers — all first class, in a 1 to 1 ratio with the solicitous crew.

The *Arandora Star* soon established a pattern of well patronised seasonal cruises from Southampton, taking in the West Indies, West Africa and Mediterranean as well as summer tours of Scandinavia. On this card issued by the company for use "on board the world's most delightful cruising liner", her handsome appearance is well set off against Norwegian mountains.

She occasionally made shorter trips. In 1931 a day cruise from Southampton to the Isle of Wight and Bournemouth was offered for 35 shillings; longer luxury cruises cost as many guineas. Taken over as a troopship in 1939, she was torpedoed the following July, with loss of 805 lives, while taking enemy internees to Canada.

1181 C. R. Hoffmann. Southampton   SOUTHERN RLY. CO.'S CROSS CHANNEL STEAMER "DINARD."

In 1923 the various private railway companies were merged into the 'Big Four': the LSWR was incorporated into the Southern Railway, which the following year took delivery of two new steamers, the *St. Briac* and the *Dinard*. Built on the Clyde in the Denny yard, at 2,300 tons they were then the largest vessels in the SR fleet, both being used on the Southampton-St. Malo service. Rodney Baker allows himself to recall that for a number of years up to 1938 his grandfather commanded the *Dinard* — here shown on a Hoffmann card of about 1930.

In 1940 she became a hospital carrier ship, which rescued 371 wounded men from Dunkirk and also served as a floating hospital for merchant seamen from vessels sunk by enemy aircraft. Equipped to take 220 patients, with a medical staff of 59, the *Dinard* served as a hospital ship off the Anzio and Normandy beaches. In June 1944 she hit a mine and had to be towed back to Southampton for repairs, after which she resumed duty, to carry back a total of 6,700 wounded servicemen on 37 trips across the Channel by the end of the year.

After the war the *Dinard* was converted to a car ferry, which operated from Folkestone. She was sold out of the railway fleet in 1958, to continue under Finnish ownership as the *Viking* until the early 1970s.

Cards like this publicised the new paddle steamer introduced on the Solent scene by Red Funnel Steamers in June 1936. They featured an inset portrait of Gracie Fields, who herself named the ship, rendering "Sing as we go" when launching her from Thornycroft's yard at Woolston on April 8th, 1936.

The *Gracie Fields*, 393 tons, had a car deck and did tender and Cowes packet service as well as excursions, for which she quickly became a favourite.

She was involved in an unusual collision on July 15th, 1939 when an RAF flying boat from Calshot struck her foremast and lost a wing as it crashed alongside her at the entrance to Southampton Water. The *Gracie Fields* was taking holiday-makers to Ryde; they were showered with pieces of metal but happily escaped injuries.

In September 1939 the *Gracie Fields* was requisitioned, to become a Dover minesweeper. On May 28th, 1940 she made a successful run to Dunkirk to pick up troops from the beaches. Returning next day, she took off another 750 men but on her way back she was dive-bombed, struck amidships and disabled. Most of those aboard her were saved by other vessels, including HMS *Pangbourne*, which took her in tow, but the Gracie Fields sank a few hours later.

Most Red Funnel steamers were taken for naval duties in the two Wars — 9 in the First, 7 in the Second.

1144 C. R. Hoffmann, Southampton.   NORTH GERMAN LLOYD S.S. "BREMEN."   51,656 TONS.   LENGTH 939 FEET.   BREADTH 103 FEET.

1143 C. R. Hoffmann, Southampton.   NORTH GERMAN LLOYD S.S. "EUROPA."   51,656 TONS.   LENGTH 939 FEET.   BREADTH 103 FEET.

The German shipping lines NDL and HAPAG, which had a very strong presence in the North Atlantic before 1914, lost almost all their liners to the victorious Allies but in the 1920s, they staged an impressive comeback — exemplified by the two liners depicted on these 1930 Hoffmann cards.

Building up its fleet again to challenge Cunard and White Star on services to New York, the NDL line ordered a pair of new 50,000 tonners, the *Europa* and the *Bremen*, launched from Hamburg and Bremen yards within a day of each other in August 1928. The former was delayed by a fire while fitting out, so the *Bremen* made her appearance first, calling at Southampton on her maiden voyage in July 1929. This she triumphantly accomplished at 27.83 knots, then returned even faster, to regain the Blue Riband for Germany, ending the supremacy of the veteran *Mauretania*.

The rebuilt *Europa* eventually came into service in March 1930, also calling at Southampton. From her maiden voyage, she held the record for a westbound crossing for three years, until it was bettered by the *Bremen*'s 28.5 knots in 1933 — and by the Italian *Rex* the same year, before the *Normandie* and *Queen Mary* dominated the Blue Riband stakes.

The postcard caption gave the *Europa* the same tonnage as the *Bremen*, 51,156, whereas she was actually some 2,000 tons less. Although not exactly sisters, the two liners were very similar in their powerful and rakish streamlined appearance — long and sleek, with rounded stems, and the first to have bulbous bows below the waterline, now a standard feature of ship design.

The NDL liners made news with a novel sea and air service to speed mail deliveries. A day or more out of port, a Lufthansa seaplane was shot into the air from a powerful catapult fixed between the funnels (visible in the photograph of the *Bremen*) but these arrangements proved costly and cumbersome and were given up in 1935.

Each with capacity for 2,000 passengers and a crew of 960, the *Bremen* and *Europa* ran a successful two-ship transatlantic service until 1939; although they lost customers after Hitler's advent to power in 1933, services were continued as subsidised symbols of German nationalism.

The liners had been kept conspicuous by having their names illuminated at night but on the outbreak of war the *Bremen* made a dramatic blacked-out dash from New York to Murmansk, then along the Norwegian coast to reach her home port in December 1939. There she was adapted as a military carrier, supposedly to transport troops to invade Britain, but she was used only as an accommodation ship, until gutted by fire in March 1941 and afterwards broken up.

The *Europa* remained at Bremerhaven when war began. She was likewise adapted as a potential carrier of invasion forces but nothing came of these preparations, nor of plans to turn her into an aircraft carrier. Surviving the war, neglected and rusting, she was temporarily repaired for brief service as a U.S. transport, then handed over to France, to undergo extensive restoration and emerge as the *Liberté* (page 89).

The *Queen Mary,* greatest of the Thirties breed of super-liners, must surely be the most celebrated and best-loved of all British ships, still known and identifiable to millions, even though they may never have seen her, much less travelled aboard her.

Her statistics alone indicate greatness — 1,018 ft. overall length, with a beam of 118 ft.; an original tonnage of 80,774, later increased to 81,237; twelve decks accommodating over 2,100 passengers and 1,000 crew; 27 boilers powering geared turbines to drive four huge propellors, which enabled her to make 31 knot crossings in 1938 that held the Blue Riband for 14 years.

In 1936, the *Queen Mary* was much more than a set of impressive statistics, she was a national symbol of optimism and pride in achievement, as Britain recovered from the depression which had delayed her building and allowed the French *Normandie* to gain a year's precedence. The keel of "No. 534" — the first major liner ordered by Cunard since the pre-war *Aquitania* — was laid at John Brown's Clydebank yard in December 1930 but trade conditions caused work to be suspended a year later. It did not resume until early in 1934, after the government agreed to grant £5 million for completion — conditional on the merging of Cunard and White Star into a single company.

Its postcard publicity included this imaginative printing by William McDowell of "Britain's Masterpiece as she would appear if placed across Trafalgar Square". giving a vivid impression of the size of the *Queen Mary.*

The launching and christening of the *Queen Mary* by Her Majesty herself on September 26th, 1934 was the first time a merchant vessel received such royal honours — indicative of her special national significance. Queen Mary and other members of the Royal family visited Southampton in May 1936 to inspect the completed liner.

Her arrival at Southampton from the Clyde on March 27th was well publicised and acclaimed. She was accompanied by a flotilla of small craft, flying all manner of welcoming flags, while many thousands lined the shore to see and admire the ocean giant. This "real photograph" card (one of the "Sun Ray" series from publishers identified only by the initials "T. & C.B.") shows the *Queen Mary* passing the *Windsor Castle* and *Majestic* beside the Western Docks on her way to the King George V Graving Dock, which had been purpose-built for her. The card is captioned "Her Maiden Voyage" but not properly so, for she is not flying the Cunard flag; she was not taken over by the company until May 12th.

The *Queen Mary* started her real maiden voyage to New York on the afternoon of May 27th. She did not at first seek to break the records set by the *Normandie* in 1935 but in August she beat the French times in both directions. After losing the Blue Riband to the *Normandie* in 1937, she regained it for both east and westbound crossings in 1938, to retain it until outpaced by the *United States* in 1952.

1268 C. R. Hoffmann, Southampton.
CUNARD WHITE STAR LINER "QUEEN MARY."
The World's Largest and Fastest Liner.
MAIN CABIN SHOPPING CENTRE.
80,773 Tons.

1275 C. R. Hoffmann, Southampton.
CUNARD WHITE STAR LINER "QUEEN MARY."
The World's Largest and Fastest Liner.
CABIN DINING SALOON.
80,773 Tons.

Before the *Queen Mary* left Southampton on her maiden voyage she was put on show to the public. Hundreds of thousands paid five shillings (today's 25p but then a lot of money, a day's pay for many workers) to go aboard and tour her sumptuously spacious accommodation. They must have been impressed, for although her layout and décor may have lacked the 'elan' and 'chic' of the *Normandie*, the liner was plentifully endowed with the best craftsmanship of the Thirties, which gave her real style. Combining glamour, prestige and luxury, 'The Mary' displayed a distinctive personality, which inspired lasting affection among those who worked and travelled on her.

Illustrated here are two of the dozen Hoffmann cards depicting her most luxurious public rooms, reserved for 'cabin' passengers — another name for first class.

Visitors in 1936 must have been surprised to enter a large shopping centre, which included familiar High Street names like W.H. Smith and Austin Reed. They would also have noted the abundance of panelling and veneers throughout the ship, for which some fifty different woods had been obtained from all parts of the Empire — modern fire regulations would not allow such profusion of timber.

Beyond the shops, the *Queen Mary* sported the full range of facilities appropriate to a 'floating palace' — lounges, bars, dining saloons, ballroom, gymnasium, swimming pool and library, not forgetting a children's playroom.

The Cabin Dining Saloon was probably the largest room afloat. Situated on 'C' deck, it was 143 ft. long and extended the full width of the ship, providing a magnificent arena to seat 815 people. Colonnaded, with subdued lighting, its show-piece was a decorative map of the North Atlantic, displaying a crystal model of the liner in its current position. If this lavish setting was not exclusive enough for the sophisticated 'upper crust' passengers, they could pay extra to eat in the Verandah Grill in the aftermost deck-house, adorned with elegant murals, red starry curtains and black carpets.

Very different were the messing arrangements aboard the grey-painted *Queen Mary* after she left New York in 1940 for conversion at Sydney into a troopship. She first operated between Australia and Suez, then returned to the North Atlantic in 1942, running a shuttle service with the *Queen Elizabeth* to carry some 15,000 American servicemen at a time to Scottish ports. Her record was 16,683 in July 1943. On these wartime voyages, the liner sailed unescorted at top speed, on a zig-zag course to avoid submarine attacks. In a tragic mishap in 1942 she sliced in half the cruiser *Curacoa* off the Irish coast and could not stop to render aid; all but 26 of the cruiser's 364 crew were drowned.

Released from trooping in September 1946, the *Queen Mary* was refitted on the Clyde, to return to commercial service; she began her first post-war Cunard voyage from Southampton on July 31st, 1947.

1247 C. R. Hoffmann, Southampton. CIE GENERALE TRANSATLANTIQUE "NORMANDIE." 79,280 TONS
The Largest Liner in the World.

1250 C. R. Hoffmann, Southampton. C.G.T. S.S. "NORMANDIE." 79,280 Tons
1st CLASS DINING SALOON.

For many transatlantic travellers, the *Normandie* represented the ultimate in ocean travel, epitomising the heights of French elegance, luxury and technology. These Hoffmann cards were issued soon after she made her maiden voyage from Le Havre to New York at the end of May 1935, calling at Southampton. She did not enter the docks but anchored off the Isle of Wight; 6 or 7 tenders carried passengers and baggage to and from her.

Four years in the building at St. Nazaire, completed a year ahead of the *Queen Mary*, the *Normandie* was indeed "the largest liner in the world" − initially of 79,280 tons, increased to 83,423 by addition of a deckhouse in 1936, to keep her ahead of the *Queen Mary*. With an overall length of 1,028 ft., she was some 10 ft. longer than the Cunard liner. Having set 30 knot records in both directions on her first round voyage, the *Normandie* was involved from 1936 in intense rivalry with the *Queen Mary*: the Blue Riband alternated between them until the latter decisively regained it in August 1938.

The postcard photograph well illustrates the unique profile of the *Normandie*. Her clipper bow and turtle-back stem graduated into a curved line of hull and superstructure which ended in an elliptical stern, while her three massive raked funnels (the aftermost one was a dummy) diminished in height moving aft, enhancing the impression of streamlined speed produced by steam turbo-electric engines geared to a quadruple screw.

Although the size and speed of the *Normandie* were impressive enough, her greatest impact was in terms of spacious luxury and elaborate decorative schemes. The French Line engaged leading French artists to create imaginative effects, sparing no expense to impress its customers, especially rich Americans. The *Normandie* had accommodation for 1,970 passengers, 850 of them in first class − 43%, a higher proportion than in any other liner.

Their dining room was the largest afloat; slightly larger than the Hall of Mirrors at Versailles, rising through three decks, it extended 300 ft., with places for up to 1,000. Exclusivity was ensured by door-guarding footmen wearing powdered wigs. A staff of 200 chefs provided high-class French cuisine.

Each first class cabin had its own distinctive décor. The main public rooms were lavishly embellished with glass and bronze work, giving a white and gold effect. The *Normandie* boasted the first real theatre (380 seats) incorporated into an ocean liner, as well as a large swimming pool, a winter garden with exotic caged birds − and much more, including a separate dining room for servants accompanying the pampered passengers.

The liner had her own special aroma of French perfume and cigarettes, which remained an abiding memory of voyages aboard her. These ended abruptly on the outbreak of war when she was laid up at New York. She was taken over by the United States in December 1941 and renamed USS *Lafayette,* but the following February she caught fire and sank during conversion as a troopship. She was salvaged but proved beyond economic repair, going for scrap in 1946.

KONINKLIJKE ROTTERDAMSCHE LLOYD

Affectionately known as "The Darling of the Dutch", the country's biggest liner, the *Nieuw Amsterdam* was also a favourite with Southampton ship-watchers, who were saddened when she was withdrawn in 1973 after 35 years of varied service in peace and war.

This aerial photograph, issued by the Holland-America Line to publicise her with the slogan "it's good to be on a well-run ship", shows her in the colours of her later years. Launched at Rotterdam in 1937 by Queen Wilhelmina, she made her maiden voyage from there to New York in May 1938, via Southampton. The Holland-America Line had started calling at the port in 1923 and continued doing so until the early Seventies.

Following her predecessor of 1906-32, the *Nieuw Amsterdam* was named after the early Dutch settlement which became New York when taken by the British in 1664. The flagship of her line, she was a graceful vessel of over 36,000 tons, powered by steam turbines, with cabins for some 1,200 passengers in three classes: she quickly gained their loyalty by the elegance of her interiors and the quality of cuisine and service offered aboard.

Remaining at New York on the outbreak of war, she was taken over by the British in 1940 and used for trooping. With commendable exactitude, her voyages over the next six years were recorded as covering 530,452 miles, carrying 378,361 servicemen on world-wide journeys. The Dutch liner received an emotional welcome when she returned to Rotterdam in April 1946. After refitting (partly at Southampton) she resumed transatlantic service in October 1947. She was later modernised and adapted for cruising.

The other major Dutch shipping company using Southampton over the years was Royal Rotterdam Lloyd (KRL). The vessel featured on this unusual card is the only one illustrated in this book which still calls at the port, albeit only occasionally and in a very different guise.

She was laid down at Flushing early in 1939 but her building was disrupted during the German occupation. It resumed after Liberation, leading to her launching in 1946, when she was named *Willem Ruys* — after a former KRL director, who had been taken hostage and executed by the Germans in reprisal for Resistance attacks.

This 21,000 ton diesel-powered liner had a distinctive silhouette, enhanced by the company's black, grey and white colour scheme. She made her maiden voyage in 1947, via Southampton, to the Dutch East Indies, via Suez, Ceylon and Singapore, continuing on this route until 1957. After modernisation, she then ran a round-the-world service going on to Australia, New Zealand, Panama and U.S. East Coast ports.

The *Willem Ruys* made her last call at Southampton in Dutch colours in 1964, after which she was sold to the Flotta Lauro line of Italy, to undergo major refitting and emerge as the *Achille Lauro*. She was first used for voyages to Australia but soon became a permanent cruise liner, distinguished by her blue-painted hull.

On this publicity card of the Fifties, her original owners were content to reproduce a painting of the *Willem Ruys* in small size on half the address side, leaving the back entirely blank for correspondence, in the style of foreign 'postal stationery' cards.

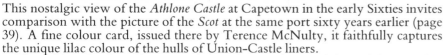

This nostalgic view of the *Athlone Castle* at Capetown in the early Sixties invites comparison with the picture of the *Scot* at the same port sixty years earlier (page 39). A fine colour card, issued there by Terence McNulty, it faithfully captures the unique lilac colour of the hulls of Union-Castle liners.

The *Athlone Castle* and her sister ship *Stirling Castle* were delivered from Belfast in 1936, to serve the faster schedules of that year's new mail contract. The two diesel-engined 25,000 ton vessels had a service speed of 20 knots. Successfully spaning the design divide of World War II, stylistically they always looked up-to-date.

The *Athlone Castle* inaugurated the new 14-day service to the Cape when she sailed from Southampton on December 22nd, 1938 — a Thursday afternoon instead of the traditional Friday departure. Two years earlier, the *Stirling Castle,* on her maiden voyage from Southampton, had broken the *Scot's* 1893 record with a passage to Capetown in 13 days 9 hours.

The liners had accommodation for 240 first class and 480 cabin passengers, but from 1940 as troopships they carried up to 6,000 men at a time, to the Middle East and later across the Atlantic. Post-war voyages to Australia with British brides and emigrants (the *Stirling Castle* also took the English Test cricketers in 1946), were followed by return to commercial duties in 1947, resuming services to South Africa.

The *Athlone Castle* made her last arrival at Southampton on August 6th, 1965. Ten days later she left for a breakers' yard in Taiwan. The *Stirling Castle* went to a similar end in Japan the next year.

The 33,532 ton liner *America,* built for the United States Lines at Newport News, was launched by Mrs. Eleanor Roosevelt on August 31st, 1939. Completed the following July, she was then unable to undertake the transatlantic crossings for which W.F. Gibbs had designed her and was initially put to cruising in the Caribbean. After Pearl Harbour, she was commissioned as USS *West Point,* to spend five years on extensive trooping duties, carrying eight times as many personnel as her original passenger capacity of 1,046, some 350,00 in all.

As such, she first called at Southampton in 1945. After reconditioning, she took up her intended role in November 1946, making regular voyages from New York to Le Havre and Southampton, at first on her own and from 1952 on a two-ship service with the more celebrated *United States* (page 93). This fine American coloured card shows the *America* being manoeuvred by the Ocean Terminal about 1960. In appearance she was typical of U.S. liners of her time, with distinctive raked and winged funnels — echoing motor car designs then in favour.

In 18 years the *America* carried nearly half a million passengers on 288 transatlantic voyages, the last of them in November 1964. She was then sold to the Chandris Group of Greece, which gave her a new life as the *Australis,* running a one-class service and cruises to Australia and round the world, starting from Southampton. After 11 years of these duties, she left the port for the last time to Australia on November 18th, 1977. Her subsequent complex career did not involve Southampton.

CUNARD WHITE STAR LINER "QUEEN ELIZABETH"
THE WORLD'S LARGEST LINER
LENGTH 1031 FT.   HEIGHT FROM MAST-HEAD TO WATER LINE 234 FT.   FROM TOP OF FORWARD FUNNEL TO WATER LINE 180FT.   TONNAGE 83,673.
SPEED EXCEEDING 16 KNOTS.   THE LARGEST AND FASTEST SHIP IN THE WORLD.   ACCOMMODATION FOR OVER 5,000 PASSENGERS
NUMBER OF DECKS 14.   LAUNCHED BY HER MAJESTY THE QUEEN 27TH SEPTEMBR 1938.

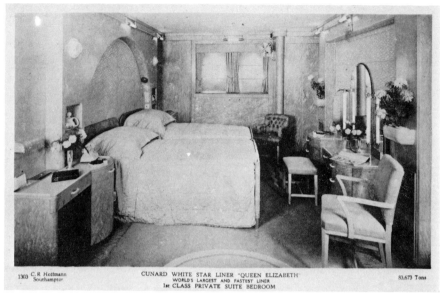

CUNARD WHITE STAR LINER "QUEEN ELIZABETH"
WORLD'S LARGEST AND FASTEST LINER   83,673 Tons
1st CLASS PRIVATE SUITE BEDROOM

The world's largest liner (83,673 gross tons, 1,031 ft. long), the *Queen Elizabeth* was laid down in December 1936 at the same Clydebank yard where the *Queen Mary* was built. Launched in September 1936 by Queen Elizabeth, she was designed as her running mate for a two-ship express service between Southampton and New York, originally planned to start in the Spring of 1940.

The outbreak of war led to her first voyage being made from the Clyde to New York in March 1940 — in great secrecy, the Germans being fed the misleading story that she was headed for dry dock completion at Southampton. Her outfitting was continued at New York and at the end of the year she left for Singapore to be converted into a troopship. As such, she shared duties in the Indian Ocean and Atlantic with the *Queen Mary* (page 77).

Embarking homeward bound American troops, the 'Queens' called at Southampton from August 1945 but not until June 1946 did the *Queen Elizabeth* come to be fitted out for her long awaited maiden voyage as a Cunard-White Star Liner. Amid great enthusiasm, she left the port on October 16th.

This Hoffmann card issued about that time gave a good impression of her power and elegance. Its detailed caption acclaimed her as "the largest and fastest ship in the world" (but she was never to run faster than the *Queen Mary*) and stated that her 14 decks had "accommodation for over 5,000 passengers" — an obvious error corrected to 2,288 on the next edition. They were served by a crew of nearly 1,300.

Back in service together, the 'Queens' proved the most successful liners on the North Atlantic runs, earning profits of over £100,000 on each voyage in 1949 and nearly always sailing fully booked. To occupy a "first class suite bedroom" on the *Queen Elizabeth*, intending passengers needed to pay a deposit well in advance. There was no shortage of takers, with a regular procession of the rich and famous travelling on the 'Queens' through the Fifties, when Cunard carried a third of all Atlantic Ocean passengers.

This Hoffmann card was one of a baker's dozen illustrating the post-war accommodation of the *Queen Elizabeth*, which generally followed the pattern of her sister ship. Most of her interiors had been worked up before the war but not fitted until 1946; they were in a more restrained style than those of the *Queen Mary* but were nevertheless opulent enough to impress passengers, who were regaled with lavish menus, in marked contrast to the rationing and shortages still affecting Britain. It was all very different from war-time conditions, when a two-berth cabin housed up to twenty GIs, sleeping in shifts in tiered bunks as many as 5 or 6 high!

The *Queen Elizabeth* operated profitably until the early Sixties, when air travel had slashed her clientele. Turning over to cruising (for which she was not really suited) did not stop her losses escalating and she was withdrawn in 1968, eventually to end her career burned out at Hong Kong in 1972.

S.S. QUEEN MARY AND QUEEN ELIZABETH.   C.M.5003.

THE QUEEN MARY FROM HYTHE SHORE ROAD.

This photograph of the 'Queens' back together in Southampton after the war was issued without an imprint but its style and serial number indicate the same publisher as the 1936 card of the *Queen Mary* illustrated on page 76.

For five of the momentous years between the two pictures, the two liners had made a major contribution to the Allied war effort, Winston Churchill's assessment was that they had jointly helped to shorten the war in Europe by at least a year. As he said, "Built for the arts of peace and to link the Old World with the New, the 'Queens' have challenged the fury of Hitlerism in the Battle of the Atlantic. At a speed never before realised in war they carried over a million men to defend the liberties of civilisation. Often, whole divisions at a time were moved by each ship. To the men who contributed to the success of our operations in the years of peril . . . the world owes a debt that it will not be easy to measure."

The great partnership of the 'Queens' lasted until 1967, when 'The Mary' was retired after making over 1,000 Atlantic crossings. The growth of air travel had undermined her viability, which cruising from 1963 failed to bolster. Her final voyage from Southampton on October 31st, 1967, on a delivery cruise to become a Californian tourist attraction, was a poignant and nostalgic occasion; thousands gathered, moist-eyed, to watch the departure of their favourite liner, so long identified with the port.

This anonymous card of the late Thirties offers a nostalgic view of the

Queen Mary off the Hythe shore, with two vintage cars in the foreground and, more significantly, three flying boats to be seen on the water, dwarfed by the giant liner. Their juxtaposition gave a prophetic sign of developments in air travel that within two post-war decades would supersede the great ocean liners, albeit with planes flying between land-based airports rather than using the sea as a natural runway.

Aircraft production had begun at the Supermarine works at Woolston before World War I. In the Twenties, production of Schneider Trophy winners and military aircraft was accompanied by progress in commercial flying boats, which initially operated from Woolston, the country's first marine airport. Supermarine joined with other companies in 1924 to form Imperial Airways, which ten years later opted for flying boats rather than land-based planes to operate the extended services of the 'all up' flat rate Empire Air Mail scheme.

In 1937 its base transferred from Croydon to Hythe, with passengers ferried by fast motor boats to and from Berth 50 in Southampton docks. A year later the embarkation raft at Hythe was moved to a position near Berth 101 in the Western Docks, then again early in 1939 to a new terminal at their Millbrook end. During the inter-war years, flying boat services and the role of Southampton as a marine airport were under the control of the Harbour Board.

Flying boat services, with a new terminal at Berth 50, were briefly revived by BOAC in 1948-50. A private venture by Aquila Airways operated for some years but ceased in 1958.

THE OCEAN TERMINAL, SOUTHAMPTON DOCKS.

This aerial view of the *Quen Elizabeth* being man-oeuvred beside the Ocean Terminal was issued as a colour postcard by Southern Newspapers, probably in the late Fifties. The world's largest liner is seen needing the attendance of no less than five tugs; two of them were Red Funnel, the other three came from the Alexandra Towing Co., the two companies sharing operations in the docks.

The impressive Ocean Terminal, opened in 1950, did not long outlive the 'Queens' it was primarily meant to serve. Its users steadily diminished through the Sixties and by 1975 only the *QE2* was left. She berthed there for the last time in 1980 and was then accommodated at berths 38/39, where a new passenger/cargo "Queen Elizabeth II Terminal" had been opened by the Queen in 1966. This is now the port's principal passenger terminal.

The early post-war years saw the revival — and short-lived expansion until the mid-Fifties — of Southampton's traditional ocean-going passenger traffic. The rapid growth of long-distance air travel superseding the great liners was not, of course, foreseen in 1946, when Southern Railway planners conceived a new Ocean Terminal to replace the old 1911 sheds at berth 43/44, to speed movement of passengers on and off the 'Queens' and other liners.

The project was completed after railway nationalisation in 1948 and opened on July 31st, 1950 by the Prime Minister, Clement Attlee, who acclaimed "this magnificent building" as "a monument to British craftsmanship", revolutionising standard of quayside passenger handling.

The Ocean Terminal was featured on many postcards, such as this one issued by Dearden & Wade of Bournemouth, which highlights the Art Deco 80 ft. tall, semi-circular tower at the southern end of the 1,300 ft. long building — 300 ft. longer than the *Queen Elizabeth* alongside it. She was the first to use the new terminal for her sailing to New York on August 1st, 1950, when 1,400 passengers were processed aboard in three hours.

Intended to complement the grandeur of the great liners and impress the Americans whose dollars Britain desperately needed, the two-storey steel and concrete structure provided two pairs of spacious reception and customs halls, served by lifts, luggage conveyors and telescopic gangways. Its many facilities included a railway platform able to take two full-length boat trains at a time — and a popular sight-seeing balcony.

The Ocean Terminal, once so much admired, has completely vanished from the docks scene. Nothing came of suggestions for alternative uses, such as an exhibition hall, and in 1983 it was demolished, somewhat precipitately, with the loss of all its ornate decoration and panelling in the lounges where film stars, world leaders and millionaires once gathered.

The cleared site has served only such mundane functions as import/export vehicle parking and storage of scrap metal awaiting export. How different are the Eighties from the Fifties . . .

1291 C. R. Hoffmann,
Southampton.   **CUNARD WHITE STAR LINER "MAURETANIA."**   34.000 Tons

O W Hoffmann,
Southampton.   CUNARD LINE
R. M. S. "CARONIA"   34.183 Tons

After the demise of the first *Mauretania* (page 51), the Cunard-White Star management preserved her famous name by having it temporarily transferred to the Red Funnel paddle steamer *Queen*, which held it until it was taken up again for the second *Mauretania*, launched in 1938.

This 35,700 ton product of the Cammell Laird yard at Birkenhead was powered by a steam turbine giving 28 knots and had capacity for some 1,100 passengers. Depicted here on a 1939 Hoffmann card, she was for Southampton essentially a post-war ship. From July 1939 she made a few trips to New York but after the outbreak of war her next voyage from there was through the Panama Canal to Sydney for conversion into a troopship. She carried many Australian soldiers to Egypt and later ferried American troops across the Atlantic.

Ending strenuous trooping service in September 1946, the *Mauretania* underwent a refit and resumed Atlantic service from Southampton in 1947. She continued in this role until 1957, when she was air-conditioned as an added facility for the cruise market, in which she was increasingly engaged − first with a white hull, then with it painted light green. Although an important 'dollar earner', she became uneconomic for Cunard and was withdrawn in 1965, leaving Southampton that November on her last voyage to the breakers.

The second *Maretania* was always dwarfed and over-shadowed by the 'Queens' but she could at least be claimed, until the launching of the *Oriana* in 1960, as the largest passenger liner built in England.

The *Caronia* revived the name of an earlier Cunard vessel of 1903-32. At 34,183 tons, she was nearly twice the size of her predecessor, launched from John Brown's Clydebank yard on October 30th, 1947 and named by the then Princess Elizabeth. A year later, the Duke of Edinburgh was aboard her for a trial run to Southampton.

Distinguished as the world's largest single-funnelled vessel, the *Caronia* was designed for double duty as an Atlantic liner and a cruise ship. Her maiden voyage from Southampton to New York on January 4th, 1949 was followed by a number of Atlantic crossings but her main role was as Cunard's first permanent prestige cruise ship − known as the 'Green Goddess' because her hull was painted a distinctive pale green. This postcard photograph of her was issued with both C.R. and O.W. Hoffmann imprints in the early Fifties.

Although a familiar sight in Southampton, the *Caronia* spent long periods away from the port, many of her cruises being based on New York. She was one of the country's biggest 'dollar earners', very popular with Americans. Nevertheless, the reduction of the Cunard fleet led to her being sold off in 1968.

She became the *Columbia* and later the *Caribia* but did not fulfil the hopes of her new owners. While being towed to a Taiwan scrapyard in 1974, she ran into heavy weather off Guam, hit a breakwater, broke in three and sank.

1313 C.R. Hottmann Southampton   SHAW SAVILL LINER "NEW AUSTRALIA"   20,256 Tons
RECONSTRUCTED BY JOHN THORNYCROFT & Co. Ltd. SOUTHAMPTON

1309 C.R. Hoffmann Southampton   R. M. L. ANDES   25,675 Tons   ROYAL MAIL LINES COPYRIGHT

"Reconstructed by John Thornycroft & Co. Ltd., Southampton" is the caption on this postcard photograph of the 20,256 ton Shaw Savill liner *New Australia*. The last (1313) in the main C.R. Hoffmann numbered series, it was probably issued soon after the re-named vessel left Southampton on her maiden voyage on August 15th, 1950.

She was originally the *Monarch of Bermuda*, built in 1931 by Vickers Armstrong for the Furness Withy service between the United States and Bermuda. Back on Tyneside in 1947, she was burnt out while refitting after war service. Taken over by the Ministry of Transport, she was virtually rebuilt in 1948-50, to carry 1,580 tourist class passengers on £10 'assisted passage' runs for emigrants to Australia (the so-called 'ten pound tourists') she also did trooping duties to Korea and Suez.

During these years she was operated by Shaw Savill on behalf of the Australian government. When her charter ended in 1957 she was laid up at Southampton until sold in 1958 to the Greek Line, becoming the *Arkadia*; her varied career ended in a Spanish breakers' yard in 1966.

As originally built, the vessel had three funnels, although the third was a dummy. It and the first disappeared during reconstruction, which retained only the centre funnel (with its distinctive Thornycroft cowl design); the boiler uptakes of the former first funnel were taken through a tripod mast substitute.

Mention of the Royal Mail line to many older Southampton folk will often evoke memories of the *Andes*. Both as buff-funnelled, black-hulled liner on South American service and as white-hulled cruise ship, she was a regular user of the port throughout her commercial life.

Her first commercial voyage started from Southampton on January 22nd, 1948 — nearly nine years late! She was scheduled to make her maiden voyage on September 26th, 1939, highlighting celebrations of the centenary of the Royal Mail company, but war intervened. Her first voyage was actually made in December 1939, from Liverpool to Halifax, Nova Scotia, to bring to Britain the first contingent of 4,000 Canadian troops. For the next six years she made trooping voyages around the world, before being refitted for her intended role.

Depicted here on a Hoffmann card of 1948, the 26,000 ton *Andes* was a product of Harland & Wolff's yard at Belfast. She had a large refrigerated capacity as well as accommodation for over 500 passengers (first and second class only), served by nearly as many crew. Dubbed the 'Queen of the South Atlantic', the largest and fastest Royal Mail passenger ship, she was much admired for her graceful lines and handsome interiors.

The *Andes* continued on the traditional route to Brazil and Argentina (also running winter cruises) until 1959, when for good economic reasons she was converted into a permanent one-class luxury cruise liner. As such, she proved very popular throughout the Sixties. Eventually, her age caught up with her; after 31 years, during which she sailed 2.75 million miles, she was withdrawn in 1971 and sent to a Belgian scrapyard.

1245 C. R. Hoffmann Southampton.   SHAW, SAVILL & A. Co's. R.M.S. "AKAROA." 15,128 Tons.

1292 C. R. Hoffmann Southampton.   SHAW SAVILL & ALBION CO'S DOMINION MONARCH.   26,500 Tons.

Ships of the Shaw, Savill and Albion line first called at Southnampton in 1914, to disembark passengers from Australia, New Zealand and South Africa. Although its fleet was primarily London-based, the company increasingly used Southampton during the inter-war years.

Its ownership or controlling interests were complex, involving at various times White Star, Ellerman and Royal Mail, which led to vessels being transferred between different fleets.

An example was the 15,128 ton *Akaroa*, built at Belfast in 1914 as the *Euripides* for the Aberdeen Line. In 1932 she was refitted and transferred to Shaw Savill for use on a service from Southamptom to New Zealand via Panama. This Hoffmann card of the early Thirties — probably deriving from a company publicity photograph — shows her in a splendid location, which gives a strong impression of New Zealand, perhaps Otago Heads.

The *Akaroa* went through the war and in 1947 resumed the service for which she had been built, continuing until 1954. She was then withdrawn, having been afloat for forty years. She had proved a great favourite on the New Zealand route, voyaging over two million miles.

The *Akaroa* and other older Shaw Savill vessels were replaced by the *Southern Cross*, which set striking new trends in modern liner design. From 1955 (when her first three outward voyages were fully booked in advance) she became a familiar sight at Southampton, until withdrawn in 1971 and sold for cruising, to be renamed *Calypso* — under which name she sometimes revisited the port.

Her distinctive, somewhat massive, profile made the *Dominion Monarch* — another fine Hoffmann subject — noteworthy among the many liners seen at Southampton. Built on Tyneside by Swan Hunters, this 26,432 ton motor ship was then the largest of her type in the world. Designed to carry 500 passengers, all first class, in great style to Australia and New Zealand via South Africa, she left on her maiden voyage from Southampton on February 17th, 1939.

Ship lovers 'down under' had little opportunity to admire her. On her third voyage this service was interrupted by the outbreak of war, ushering in seven years of arduous duty as a troopship, during which she carried a total of 90,000 servicemen around the world . . . after escaping from Singapore only minutes ahead of the advancing Japanese.

The *Dominion Monarch* returned to Shaw Savill service in 1948, after a major overhaul by her original builders. She continued until 1961, when escalating operating costs brought the decision to withdraw her. Her last commercial voyage from Southampton started on December 30th, finishing back at her home port on April 20th, 1962, when she received siren salutes all round. She was afterwards briefly chartered for use as a hotel ship during the World's Fair at Seattle, then sent to Japan for scrapping.

No 1176. C. R. Hoffmann, Southampton   R.M.M.V. "WINCHESTER CASTLE."   20,109 Tons.

UNION-CASTLE LINE TO SOUTH AND EAST AFRICA.

THE UNION-CASTLE ROYAL MAIL MOTOR VESSEL "WINCHESTER CASTLE."   20,001 TONS.

The 20,000 ton Union-Castle liner *Winchester Castle* was familiar in Southampton in two different forms, both before and after World War II.

This Hoffmann card, issued soon after she came into service in 1930, shows her with the classic profile of a Harland & Wolff motorship, with two funnels. The amount of smoke coming from them looks curious — perhaps resulting from some imaginative touching up of a photograph to give a supposedly more realistic impression of a liner at sea, as was not infrequently done for pre-war shipping cards.

The *Winchester Castle* made her maiden voyage from Southampton to the Cape in October 1930. She had capacity for about 250 passengers in three classes plus some 200,000 cubic feet of refrigerated storage; the Union-Castle company increasingly used its mail ships for importing South African fruit and other produce.

In 1938 the *Winchester Castle* was re-engined to increase her power and enable her to make 14-day voyages to the Cape, whereas previously she had taken 16 days. As can be seen from the accompanying company publicity card, she also benefited visually from this rebuilding. Her original two squat funnels were replaced by a single raked low one, giving her a more streamlined and elegant appearance, in keeping with later vessels of the Union-Castle fleet, although she retained the straight stem which identified her origin.

During the war the *Winchester Castle* served as a troop carrier and assault vessel. She spent a year in Scottish waters as a training ship for assault troops and later took part in landings in North Africa, Sicily, Italy and France.

Having covered some 270,000 miles on wartime duties, she then made several trips to South Africa carrying emigrants before being returned to Union-Castle in 1948 for refitting. This did not affect her external appearance but altered her accommodation to 186 first class and 400 tourist class berths. She resumed South African service from Southampton in September 1949, operating a weekly mail schedule, along with seven other ships, to Madeira, Capetown, Port Elizabeth, East London and Durban.

This continued through the Fifties, the final 'golden age' of the famous Union-Castle service, which thereafter diminished to the point of closing down in 1977. Until then, three or more of the company's vessels could usually be seen in the port; many local ship-lovers will remember standing on the Royal Pier on a summer Thursday afternoon to watch one of these beautiful ships depart for southern climes.

The *Winchester Castle* herself did not last beyond 1960, when she was withdrawn for scrapping, after being superseded by the new *Windsor Castle*. This splendidly appointed new 38,000 ton Union-Castle flagship herself ran for only 17 years, before the company ended its operations and she sailed away to Saudi Arabia to become a leisure centre and accommodation ship for oil workers.

R.M.S. STRATHNAVER

THE 42,000 TON P. & O. - ORIENT PASSENGER LINER 'ORIANA'   5151

Ships of the Peninsular and Oriental line were the first to use the new Southampton dock in 1842 but the company ceased calling at the port in 1881 (page 10). Forty-four years later it resumed the connection. In 1925 P & O inaugurated a fortnightly cargo service to Japan and from 1929 larger passenger ships began visiting the port on cruising voyages, establishing a continuing tradition, now most notably maintained by the celebrated *Canberra*, which first arrived at Southampton in May 1961.

A famous quintet of P & O liners built in the 1930s were all given names starting with 'Strath'. The 'Straths' were designed to serve the dual purposes of regular line voyages (mainly from London) and cruises in the off-season. They were given buff funnels and white hulls, very different from the black funnels and khaki upperworks of previous P & O ships.

This pre-war card from J. Salmon Ltd. reproduced a painting by S.R. Hopkins, a fine study of the *Strathnaver* — which lost two of her original three funnels after refitting in 1950. Delivered from Vickers Armstrong's Barrow yard in 1931, she was a vessel of 22,547 tons, powered by steam turbines which gave her a speed of 21 knots.

She carried some 1,000 passengers in two classes, until 1954 when her accommodation became tourist class only. When not being used for cruising from Southampton, she served the London-Australia route — until 1961, when she was withdrawn for scrapping.

The caption on this fine aerial photograph, issued as a deckle-edged postcard by Dearden & Wade in the early 1960s, names the *Oriana* as "The 42,000 ton P & O – Orient Passenger Liner". The hyphen was significant, representing the realities of ownership since 1918, although the two companies ran as separate organisations until amalgamating in 1964.

The *Oriana* began her maiden voyage from Southampton to Australia on December 3rd, 1960. Another product of the Barrow yard, she was large and powerful, with geared turbines enabling her to make 30 knots. She reached Sydney in 27 days, knocking four days off the time taken by other liners. Along with the *Canberra* (45,733 tons), which came into service the following year, the *Oriana* was not only faster but bigger and more luxurious, showing radical advances in design and presenting a splendidly modern appearance — not at first enthusiastically accepted by everyone who saw her.

Through the Sixties the 11-deck *Oriana* made round-the-world voyages, as well as cruising, but from 1973 (like the *Canberra*) she was exclusively employed on cruises. In that capacity she carried up to 1,677 passengers (all one class), compared with her previous accommodation for over 2,000 in two classes. She proved very successful, operating from Southampton in the summer and Sydney in the winter (the Australian summer). In November 1981 she made her last departure from Southampton. After a few more years cruising from Australia she was sold in 1986 to Japanese interests, to become a floating 'cultural attraction'.

This impressive aerial view of the *Liberté* off New York, with the Statue of Liberty in the background, was issued as a postcard by the French Line (Compagnie Générale Transatlantique or Transat to the French) to publicise its Le Havre-Southampton-New York service in the Fifties.

The *Liberté* was originally the 1930 German Liner *Europa* (page 75), allocated to France in 1946 by way of compensation for the loss of the *Normandie* (page 78). That December she broke adrift at Le Havre in a gale and hit the sunken wreck of the *Paris*. After salvage, she was towed to St. Nazaire, where her restoration and refitting occupied three years. This rebuilding increased her tonnage to 51,839, making her France's largest liner until the advent of the *France* in 1961.

The *Liberté* kept the massive hull and superstructure of the *Europa* but her new funnels helped to give her a distinctive appearance. The postcard photograph was taken after 1954, when rounded domes were fitted on top of them.

As the new flagship of the French Line, she made her maiden voyage to New York in August 1950, receiving a civic welcome and send-off at Southampton. The *Liberté* maintained transatlantic services along with her famous running mate *Ile de France* (1927-58) and the smaller 1952 *Flandre*. In 1961 she completed her last season on the North Atlantic run and was withdrawn as her successor, the *France*, neared completion. She went to Italian breakers in 1962.

Preceding the *Normandie* (page 78), the *Ile de France* was the first French Line ship to call at Southampton, inaugurating in January 1935 an outward call here instead of at Plymouth. Built in 1929, she continued in service for 31 years, playing as important a role in the post-war fortunes of the French Line as she had during pre-war years.

This deckle-edged French postcard shows her in her post-war guise, with two funnels, after extensive rebuilding in 1947-49. Her original appearance was that of a conventional three-funnelled liner, with straight stem and counter stern, at 43,150 tons then one of the largest but not particularly fast and with little exterior hint of her exciting interiors. She was a precursor of the *Normandie* as a floating luxury resort, designed in modern French style, with a panache that greatly appealed to the wealthy and fashionable. By 1935 she had carried more first class passengers than any other transatlantic liner. They had the choice of 390 cabins, decorated in as many different styles, all with veneer panelling — which vibration caused to creak disconcertingly until padded and refixed in 1933.

The *Ile de France* was taken over by the Admiralty in 1940 and did splendid trooping service in both Eastern and North Atlantic waters, sailing under the dual flags of Britain and Free France. Handed back to her owners in 1946 and thoroughly refitted, she ran with the *Liberté* and other French Line vessels, until withdrawn in 1958. After featuring in a 'disaster movie', she was scrapped at Osaka in 1959.

1220 C. R. Hoffmann, Southampton.　　M.S. "JOHAN VAN OLDENBARNEVELT."　　19,040 TONS.

1230 C. R. Hoffmann, Southampton.　　M.S. "MARNIX VAN SINT ALDEGONDE."　　19,128 TONS.

Of all the passenger liners seen at Southampton, the Dutch sister-ships *Johan Van Oldenbarnevelt* and *Marnix Van Sint Aldegonde* can surely claim the longest names, not easily pronounced by English speakers but significant for the Dutch. These 19,000 ton motor vessels were depicted on Hoffmann cards issued in the early Thirties, soon after they came on the scene, built at Amsterdam in 1930 to the order of the Nederland Line (Stoomvaart Maatschappij "Nederland") for its old-established service to the Dutch East Indies. The company had a long connection with Southampton, its ships having started to call at the port in mid-Victorian times.

These two liners served the Dutch East Indies route until 1940, when they were put to war duties. The *MVSA* fell victim to aerial attack in 1943 but the *JVO* continued in service for another twenty years, until coming to a tragic end in 1963.

Her distinctive name was adopted in compliment to the memory of the Dutch stateman Johan Van Oldenbarnevelt (1547-1619). He was for over thirty years the virtual prime minister of Holland, the largest of the seven United Provinces of the Netherlands, unifying their fight for independence from Spain. After its successful conclusion, internal religious and constitutional disputes (he was for toleration and autonomy) led to his execution in 1619 — afterwards much regretted; he became revered as a 'founding father' of the Netherlands.

Marnix Van Sint Aldegonde took the name of the Dutch writer, Protestant theologian and statesman (1538-98), who made important contributions to Dutch literature and national identity.

The final wartime trooping voyage of the *JVO* ended at Southampton in October 1945. She was then used by the Dutch government to carry troops to the Dutch East Indies and emigrants to Australia. She underwent a major rebuilding in 1951 but with the virtual ending of the Dutch empire the liner operated on various routes as a single class ship carrying emigrants, students etc.

In 1959 she received a second and more radical rebuilding, from which she emerged with light grey hull and round-topped funnels. Her last period of Nederland service was spent on round-the-world voyages from Amsterdam and Southampton via the East, Australia, Pacific and U.S. ports.

In 1962 she was sold to the Shipping Investment Corporation of Greece and the following April re-appeared in Southampton as the *Lakonia*, to make a series of cruises to the Canary Islands. On December 19th, 1963, she left the port with 651 passengers for a Christmas cruise. Three days later fire broke out aboard her, north of Madeira. Amid confusion and rescue attempts by five other vessels which rushed to the scene, the calamity ended with 130 persons dead or unaccounted for. The *Lakonia* was then taken in tow but on December 29th she sank 250 miles west of Gibraltar.

Red Funnel Steamers   BALMORAL   Southampton

T.S.M.V. "PACIFIC COAST." - 1600 tons
Summer Coastal Cruises between Liverpool and London and vice versa, calling at Intermediate Ports.
COAST LINES, LIMITED, Royal Liver Building, Liverpool 3; and London House, New London Street, E.C.3.

Still afloat after forty years, the *Balmoral* will recall summer days and trips to the Isle of Wight for those who knew her in the Fifties and Sixties.

A product of Thornycroft's yard at Woolston, she began regular service for the Red Funnel company in December 1949, taking the name of the 1900 paddle steamer scrapped earlier that year (page 22). The second *Balmoral* was a neat, well-fitted, vessel of 688 gross tons, powered by two diesel engines which gave her a service speed of 14 knots. She had a rear car deck which doubled as a sun deck on excursions. "Passengers and Cars: Mainland to Isle of Wight: Catering Aboard" was the advertisement on the back of this Fifties publicity card.

The *Balmoral* was withdrawn from Red Funnel service in 1968 but has continued in use, running cruises for other companies and occasionally returning to Southampton and local waters.

Her passengers in the Fifties would have been impressed by the growth of the huge Esso refinery at Fawley — which is within the port of Southampton, making it a major oil port, serving installations with an annual capacity of over 19 million tons, a tenth of the U.K. total.

Begun by the AGWI company in 1921 to serve ships in the docks, the refinery was acquired by Standard Oil in 1926. It was greatly expanded in the early post-war years, with the construction of 4,200 ft. of deep water jetties, able to take five of the largest bulk carriers. Cargo handled within the port in 1962 totalled 23.6 million tons, of which oil represented over 90%. Developments at Fawley have attracted related industries and power stations, now extending along several miles of the shore.

As we write, the Town Quay is being redeveloped as a residential and leisure centre, a new use for a part of the old port that has outlived its earlier function. Until the Sixties, the Town Quay (page 24) was usually bustling with activity as small freighters and coastal vessels discharged their varied cargoes. Ships from northern Europe were often berthed there, with timber a common cargo.

Well represented among British callers were vessels of Coast Lines Ltd., a sizeable company until absorbed by others in the Sixties. They carried freight all around the British coasts and also offered "Summer Coastal Cruises between Liverpool and London and vice versa, calling at Intermediate Ports" — as advertised on this postcard, issued by B. & A. Feilden of Liverpool, where the company had its headquarters. Southampton, of course, was one of the "intermediate ports" on these voyages, which provided modest but comfortable accommodation at a cost of only a few pounds and probably gave less well-off passengers a greater experience of 'real' life afloat than some more expensive cruises on larger vessels covering longer distances abroad.

The good-looking ship depicted on the card was the 1,600 ton *Pacific Coast*, built at Ardrossan in 1935. Coast Lines stopped calling at Southampton on a regular basis in 1962.

1239 C. R. Hoffmann
Southampton.
DEUTSCHE OST-AFRIKA LINIE S.S. "UBENA."
9,554 TONS

H. M. T. EMPIRE KEN
678

Following the Second World War, as after the First, most surviving German liners were taken over as reparations by the victorious Allies and allocated amongst them, to be refitted and given new identities and roles. The French received the *Europa*, which was rebuilt as the *Liberté* (page 89); several went to the Russians, who kept some in service until quite recently.

The British share of German tonnage included five smaller vessels, which were put to duty as troopships, based at Southampton. They were given 'Empire' names − *Empire Fowey* (ex *Potsdam*); *Empire Orwell* (ex *Pretoria*); *Empire Trooper* (ex *Cap Norte*); *Empire Windrush* (ex *Monte Rosa*) and the one illustrated here, the *Empire Ken*, formerly the *Ubena*.

This Hoffmann card of the *Ubena* was issued about five years after she came into service, built in 1928 at the Blohm & Voss yard in Hamburg for the German East Africa Line. At 9,554 tons, she was a small but elegant ship, seen regularly at Southampton up to the outbreak of war, along with others of the fleet with which her owners ran a series of cargo and passenger services to and around Africa. After 1939, the company's colours were not seen again at Southampton until the Seventies, when a container ship revived the connection.

During the war, the *Ubena* served the Germany navy as a mother ship to 'U' boat flotillas. At the end of the conflict, she became one of several passenger vessels engaged in evacuating German nationals from the East, carrying over 20,000 people on seven voyages.

The *Ubena* surrendered to the British in July 1945 and was sent to Southampton for trooping duties, to be managed by Royal Mail. Renamed the *Empire Ken* − as shown on this Dearden & Wade card of about 1950 − she became a familiar sight at Southampton, until withdrawn for scrapping in 1957.

By that time, the Empire had become the Commonwealth, with many of its members gaining independence, and Britain's overseas defence commitments were diminishing, with movement by air superseding trooping by sea, 1962 saw the withdrawal of the last troopship, ending a long-lasting aspect of Southampton port activity.

Southampton has not, however, lost all its military connections. Opposite the Western Docks is the Marchwood Military Port, the Headquarters of the Royal Corps of Transport Maritime Operations. Originally built in 1943 as part of the preparations for D-Day, it subsequently expanded its facilities to include Ro-Ro capabilities through which it supplies the Army in Europe and elsewhere (including the Falklands in 1982).

Further down the estuary at Hythe is a U.S. Army Activity Base, which maintains a small fleet of tugs, barges and pontoons. This was previously the site of Supermarine seaplane construction.

Rodney Baker ruefully remembers that in July 1952 an illness deprived him of his once-in-a-lifetime chance of seeing the new holder of the Blue Riband arrive at Southampton. Others were more fortunate; tens of thousands occupied every available vantage point to watch and cheer the *United States* as she headed for the Ocean Terminal, accompanied on the last leg of her historic voyage by a veritable armada of small craft.

The warmth of Southampton's welcome surprised all aboard her, for she had wrested the coveted award from the *Queen Mary*, most beloved of British liners, which had held it since August, 1938.

The *Queen Mary* then made the eastward crossing at 31.69 knots. A century after the last American holder of the Blue Riband, the *United States* secured it by averaging 35.59 knots on her maiden voyage, covering the 2,942 nautical miles from the Ambrose lightship to Bishop Rock in 3 days, 10 hours and 40 minutes — over 10 hours faster than the *Queen Mary*. For good measure, she did the return crossing at 34.51 knots, another decisive and enduring advance on the previous record.

This anonymous "real photo" card (given to the writer by his mother in 1952) shows the *United States* berthed at the Ocean Terminal, well illustrating her sleek and powerful profile, enhanced by her huge streamlined funnels.

W. J. Nigh & Sons of Ventnor were the publishers of this handsome study (copyright, reproduced by permission) of the *United States* passing the *Queen Elizabeth* off Cowes — an evocative and nostalgic scene indeed.

Built at Newport News, Virginia, the 53,329 ton *United States* was powered by steam turbines geared to quadruple screws. She came almost at the end of the era of fast ocean liners, as the crowning achievement of her perfectionist designer, William Francis Gibbs. America's leading naval architect, he had dreamed and planned such a vessel over thirty years, as an expression of both patriotism and advanced technology.

Gibbs had been involved in salvaging the *Normandie* after her fire at New York in 1942 and had designed the most powerful fire engine as well as the fastest liner. The United States Lines got a two-thirds government subsidy for its new liner on the basis of her national defence value as a potential troopship, which reinforced Gibbs' dedication to fire prevention. He used mainly steel, aluminium and plastic, forbidding the wooden panelling and fittings that so adorned the Cunard 'Queens'.

The *United States* was built in dry dock, almost secretly; largely prefabricated, she was given a smooth hull and a rakish stem. Nearly 1,000 ft. long, she was designed to pass through the Panama Canal.

With capacity for 2,000 passengers in air-conditioned comfort, she did well in the Fifties but her trade fell off in the Sixties, in the face of growing air competition. She left Southampton for the last time in November 1969 and has been laid up ever since.

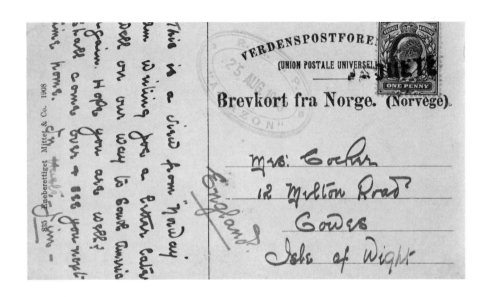

These two postcards span half a century of Southampton maritime history. Besides depicting a wide range of ships connected with the port, the cards featured in this book sometimes carry messages from people who worked aboard them, offering vivid personal sidelights on our shipping history. Many shipping cards are unused, bought as souvenirs or for collectors' albums, but the primary function of postcards has always been for correspondence, briefly expressed and cheaply sent. Older cards sometimes acquire historical significance, never envisaged by the senders who penned their few lines "in haste".

As a document of postal and maritime history, the correspondence side of this Norwegian card is more important than its picture of sunset over a cape in the north of Norway. In August 1908 Jim used it to write to a lady in Cowes "This is a view from Norway. Well on our way to South America. Hope you are well. Shall come over and see you next time home." He was evidently a crew member (perhaps Southampton-based) aboard the *Amazon*, one of the Royal Mail 'A' class ships, in service from 1906 until 1918, when she was torpedoed.

Jim must have acquired the card when she made a summer cruise to Norway, before resuming line voyages to South America. He would have handed it in at the purser's office, where the RMSP ship's handstamp was applied, dated "25 Aug. 1908". British stamps could be used on British ships and were accepted by foreign post offices where ship's mail was received at convenient ports of call — in this case probably Lisbon, judging by the 'Paquete' cancellation over the stamp, which indicates 'packet boat' or 'ship's mail'. Without further postmarking, the card was then sent to England in the normal course of international mail.

"Greetings from Southampton" has been the theme of many multi-view cards, such as this Dearden & Wade deckle-edged black and white "real photo" production, probably of the Fifties. Such cards are not much favoured by today's collectors but are popular enough with the public, providing five miniatures for the price of one standard size picture.

Southampton is here exemplified by the Royal Pier — whose entrance building is externally unaltered, although the pier itself is disused — and four liners, which no longer grace the port. The *Queen Mary*, *Queen Elizabeth* and *America* have featured on earlier pages but no space could be found for the *Capetown Castle*.

This former Union-Castle flagship, partner of the *Stirling Castle* and *Athlone Castle* (page 80), was the first of her line to be given a non-British 'castle' name. The Belfast-built 27,000 ton liner began service from Southampton to South Africa in 1938 but a year later she was taken over as a troopship. She covered half a million miles on government service, carrying American troops across the Atlantic, also lease-lend cargoes and food for Britain. The *Capetown Castle* re-opened the Southampton-South Africa mail service on January 9th, 1947 and continued on this route until withdrawn in 1967.

What four ships could one select today to symbolise Southampton? Certainly a cruise liner, the *QE2* or *Canberra*, but for the rest . . .? A container ship, a vehicle carrier and a bulk cargo vessel? Selection would be invidious, for they are all functional rather than photogenic, with little more than size and power to commend them. Alas, the days of sleek 'ocean greyhounds' and graceful 'floating palaces' are long gone . . .

The changing port scene

In the nature of things, postcards do not illustrate the manifold activities of the port during World War II, nor the many post-war changes in and around Southampton docks.

Hostilities intensified port operations to meet military supply and transport needs but these functions had to be undertaken in the face of numerous air raids of varying severity. The resulting damage had less effect than expected; port installations and services were interrupted but most soon resumed after emergency repairs and improvisation. Much ship repair work was carried out in the docks and elsewhere, while Thornycrofts built 17 destroyers and many other war craft.

Southampton was the principal embarkation point for the first expeditionary force to France in 1939-40 and the main base for the 1944 invasion fleet, which was assembled, closely packed several ships abreast, along every available quay. Much of the floating Mulberry Harbour was constructed within Southampton docks and the port was also closely involved in the PLUTO pipeline project. In all, over four million servicemen (half of them American) passed through Southampton, which handled about as many tons of military supplies during the war.

Its role as a peacetime trooping port ended in 1962 — apart from the brief revival of traditional port activity in 1982, when the requisitioned *QEII* and *Canberra* and other vessels were urgently refitted for use in the Falklands campaign.

Southampton's ocean-going passenger traffic reached its peak in the mid-Fifties, at nearly 690,000, but then declined steadily to half that number by 1974, afterwards falling more sharply to under 75,000 in the early Eighties — almost entirely for cruises. For a time, the accelerating reduction in the port's traditional long-distance liner trade was cushioned by the growth of shorter distance roll on/roll off import/export, car and passenger ferries to the Continent. After British Rail concentrated its Channel Island passenger service at Weymouth in 1961 and withdrew its Le Havre and St. Malo services in 1964, several private operators (notably Thoresen Car Ferries and P & O Normandy Ferries) came in to run cargo, coach and car ferries to France and Spain. The peak figures were reached in 1973, with 300,000 vehicles and 900,000 passengers, but traffic afterwards contracted and in 1983-84 the main operators transferred to Portsmouth, others having previously ended their services.

These developments had involved filling in the Inner Dock in 1964 and remodelling the Outer Dock in 1967, as the Princess Alexandra Dock. Since 1984 the redundant area has been developed as Ocean Village; another complex of shops, offices, houses and marina is taking shape around the Town Quay and similar developments are planned for the area between them, including the Trafalgar dry dock, closed for ship-repairing in 1988 and expected to become a marina.

The Prince of Wales dry dock was closed in 1976 and filled in a year later, to serve the vehicle trade. General cargo has been replaced by specialised traffic, mainly in cars and bulk grain, with two new export terminals built in the Eastern Docks in the early Eighties. Back in 1934, the Solent Flour Mills highlighted the beginning of the industrial estate adjoining the then new Western Docks; many more enterprises have since been established there, including the Martini Rossi storage and bottling plant, which receives wine in bulk through a pipeline erected in 1976.

Conventional cargo handled in the port in the Sixties was about 1.3 million tons a year, the total having varied little over the previous fifty years. Between 1981 and 1987 it increased from 2 to 6.6 million tons, indicative of the rapid growth of container traffic.

In 1963 responsibility for the port was transferred from the British Transport Commission to the British Transport Docks Board (from 1982 Associated British Ports); it incorporated the Southampton Harbour Board in 1968. This administrative reorganisation was related to heavy capital expenditure to create new deep water quays on reclaimed land beyond the King George V Graving Dock up to Redbridge Causeway, equipped to take the largest container vessels and served by a Freightliner rail terminal and a direct motorways link.

The first quay at the new container terminal came into use in October, 1968. The planned development, providing over 3,000 ft. of quays for five container berths and large areas for mechanised cargo handling and storage, was completed in 1978, soon named the Prince Charles Container Port.

More large ships now come to the port of Southampton (including Fawley — see page 91) than in the Thirties but they are mostly container vessels and bulk carriers, which are in port for hours rather than days, so their visible presence is not so noticeable. By their nature, they are far less interesting and attractive than the great ocean liners of yester-year, which had distinctive profiles and personalities, affectionately remembered by those fortunate enough to have seen and admired them.

In this book the maritime heritage of Southampton has necessarily been presented mainly through pictures of the docks and the liners using them, but it should not be forgotten that their handling and servicing was far less mechanised and much more labour-intensive than today, involving many thousands of people aboard them and in and around the docks, doing everything from loading and unloading, maintenance and repair, to supplying provisions, laundry and floral decorations . . . with much pride and skill.

INDEX OF SHIPS

Ship	Page(s)
Achille Lauro	79
Ada	42
Adriatic	36
Agamemnon	40
Akaroa	86
Alcantara	60,61
Alma	26
Amazon (HMS)	53
Amazon (RMSP)	94
America	80,94
Andes	61,85
Aquitania	51,55,60,63,64,66,67,76
Aragon	49
Arandora Star	60,73
Arcadia	10
Arcadian	55
Arkadia	85
Arlanza	29
Arundel Castle	50
Asturias (I)	55
Asturias (II)	61
Assaye	54
Athlone Castle	80,94
Atlantis	61
Audacious	37
Australis	80
Avon	29
Balmoral (I)	22
Balmoral (II)	91
Baltic	36
Berengaria	5,60,63,65,67,68
Bismarck	65
Bitterne	53
Blazer	45
Braemar Castle	54,55
Bremen	51,75
Britannia	10
Britannic (I)	36,48,55
Britannic (II)	62
Brussels	56
Bülow	40
Caledonia	65
Calypso	86
Cambria	22
Canberra	88,94,95
Capetown Castle	94
Caribia	84
Carnarvon Castle	73
Caronia	84
Cedric	36
Celtic	10,36
City of New York	10,34
City of Paris	34
Columbia (LSWR)	26
Columbia	84
Curacoa	77
Cutty Sark	53
Czar	58
Dane	31
Danube	28,49
Deutschland	30,40
Dinard	74
Dominion Monarch	86
Don	27
Duchesss of Fife	63
Dunbar Castle	73
Dunnottar Castle	39
Dunvegan Castle	31
Durham Castle	32
Empire Fowey/Orwell/ Trooper/Windrush	92
Empire Ken	92
Empire Penryn	58
Empress of Australia	60,71
Empress of Britain	60,71,72
Empress of Scotland	40
Eros	43
Essex Ferry	59
Estonia	58
Euripides	86
Europa	75,89
Fawley	12
Flandre	89
Floating Bridge	11,12
France	89
Frauenlob	57
Georgic	62
Gladiator	46,47
Grace Dieu	7
Gracie Fields	74
Great Eastern	10,34
Hampshire	52
Hampton	23
Hansa	30
Harvard	34
Hawke	37
Her Majesty	21
Highflyer	30
Hilda	42
Homeric	60
Hotspur	23
Ibex	41
Ile de France	89
Imperator	65,68
Johan Van Oldenbarnevelt	90
Kaiser Wilhelm der Grosse	29,30
Kaiser Wilhelm II	40
Kaiserin Auguste Victoria	40
Knightsgarth	43
Lady Brussels	56
Lafayette	78
Lakonia	90
Lark	43
Leonard	59
Leviathan	69
Liberté	75,89
Limax	59
Llangibby Castle	73
Lorna Doone	22
Lusitania	51,66
Louisville	35
Magdalena	27
Majestic	60,63-5,70,76
Marnix Van Sint Aldegonde	90
Mauretania (I)	30,51,55,60,66-7
Mauretania (II)	84
Monarch of Bermuda	85
Monticello	40
New Australia	85
New York	10,34,37,48
Nieuw Amsterdam	79
Nile	49,54
Normandie	21,75-6,78-9,89
Nubian	53
Oceana	10
Oceanic	40
Olympic	36-7,48
Oriana	84
Orinoco	27
Oruba	40
Pacific Coast	91
Pangbourne	74
Paris	21
Pathfinder	45
Plattsburg	34
Princess Daffodil	59
Princess Iris	59
Pulaski	58
Queen	84
Queen Elizabeth	67,77,81-3,93-4
Q.E. 2	83,94-5
Queen Mary	51,67,75-8,81-2,93-4
Rex	75
St. Briac	74
St. Luis	35
St. Paul	35,46-7
Saxon	32,39
Scot	39,80
Skyterren	45
Snaefell	57
Solent Queen	10,21
Southampton	57
South Western	26
Southern Cross	86
Speedwell	13
Stella	41
Stirling Castle	80,94
Strathnaver	88
Suevic	44-5
Tantallon Castle	31
Tartar	53
Teutonic	46
Tirpitz	71
Titanic	36-7,48
Train Ferry No. 4	59
Ubena	92
United States	23,69,76,80,93
Vaterland	69
Victoria	10
Victoria Luise	30
Victoria & Albert	70
Viking	74
Viper	57
Vulcan	48
Warwick Castle	73
Wavertree	53
Willem Ruys	79
Winchester Castle	73,87
Windsor Castle (I)	50,76
Windsor Castle (II)	87